STRINGING
& LINKING
JEWELRY WORKSHOP

Handcrafted designs & techniques

STRINGING & LINKING
JEWELRY WORKSHOP

Sian Hamilton

First published 2015 by
Guild of Master Craftsman Publications Ltd
Castle Place, 166 High Street, Lewes,
East Sussex BN7 1XU

Text © GMC Publications, 2015
Copyright in the Work © GMC Publications Ltd, 2015

Step photography by the jewelry designers; all other
photography by Laurel Guilfoyle.

ISBN 978-1-86108-768-3

Publisher Jonathan Bailey
Production Manager Jim Bulley
Senior Project Editor Dominique Page
Editor Ruth O'Rourke-Jones
Managing Art Editor Gilda Pacitti
Designer Ginny Zeal

Set in ITC Century BT
Color origination by GMC Reprographics
Printed and bound in China

Contents

INTRODUCTION

Jewelry making is one of the most rewarding hobbies you can have. You don't need too many expensive tools to make a start and this book is the perfect place to begin if you don't have any experience at all. The basic skills are easily learned and patience will be rewarded with beautiful jewelry you can show off to all your friends and family.

I am Sian Hamilton, and I have been making jewelry for more than 30 years. From the first string of beads I made as a child and wore with pride, through a degree in 3D design specializing in jewelry, I have been immersed in design my entire life. These days I make and sell jewelry by commission, have recently written a couple of books about jewelry making and am also the editor of a magazine for jewelry makers called *Making Jewellery*. The magazine has many amazingly talented designers creating beautiful projects. It is these designers that have created the stunning projects in this book.

Style is a very personal thing and the projects we have included in this book will appeal to a wide range of tastes. But it's always good to remember that the projects aren't set in stone. If you love red and the designer has used blue then swap to the color of your choice. Or, if the beads being used are a bit too big for you, then reduce the size of the beads and make a finer version of the piece. Projects can be used as inspiration rather than a set of instructions to follow. You may find you like parts of two different projects that you can mix together to create something completely unique. Personally, I would recommend starting with making some of the projects exactly as they are shown to build your skill level. Then you can move on to using the projects as design inspiration and have the confidence to change a few things to make the pieces different. That way you can say the jewelry design is truly yours!

Tools & Equipment

The following pages explain the basic tools and equipment that you will need to make the projects in this book. Many of the miscellaneous tools are non-specialist items available in DIY and craft shops.

PLIERS AND CUTTERS

Below are the various types of pliers and cutters that you will need as a beginner. As your skills progress, there are many specialist types that are suited to particular tasks that would be a good investment.

1 Round-nose pliers
These pliers have round jaws that taper to the end and are used for making jumprings, eyepins, loops, and spirals.

2 Chain-nose pliers
Sometimes known as snipe-nose pliers, these pliers have flat jaws that taper at the end. They are useful for holding small items such as neck ends and opening and closing jumprings.

3 Flat-nose pliers
These pliers have flat jaws that do not taper. They are used for holding wire, closing ribbon crimps, and opening and closing jumprings.

4 Side cutters
These cutters have the cutting jaw on the side—they have a pointed nose and can cut flush to your piece. The point also allows the cutters to access smaller areas.

5 Scissors
Small, sharp, pointed scissors are used for trimming cords, ribbon, thread, and cutting shrink plastic.

6 Memory-wire cutters
Specifically designed to cut memory wire, these are heavy-duty cutters. Memory wire is extremely hard and will ruin normal cutters.

7 Pinking shears
This style of scissors has wavy jaws to create a wavy pattern to the cut line.

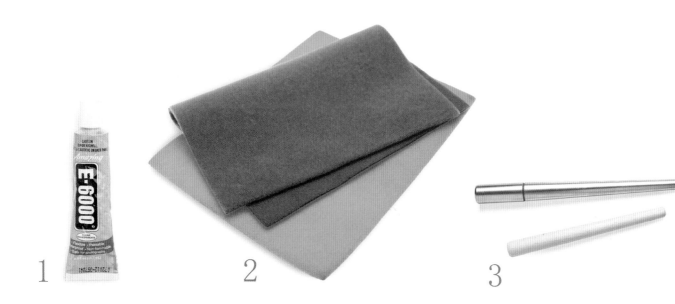

MISCELLANEOUS TOOLS

You may already have some of these useful bits of kit at home. Have a hunt around and see what you can repurpose. From a DIY hammer for flattening metal, to wooden dowels as mandrels, household items can help keep costs down when starting out.

1 Adhesive

When making jewelry, use glues that are suited to the purpose. Many cyanoacrylate glues (also known as superglue) can react with metals and melt materials, though this type of glue can be used for certain tasks. White (PVA) glue is a common glue that is often used when working with children and can be used to seal paper. Liquid cement-style glue is good for adding to knots for extra security. Industrial, thick, silicone-based glues, such as E6000, is used to coat wire to stop sharp edges from scratching skin and for sticking shrink plastic to combs and metal findings. Note: Make sure you use adhesives in a well-ventilated area.

2 Bead mats

These mats feel like velvet and have a texture that holds on to beads, and prevent them from rolling around on the work surface.

3 Mandrels

These are useful for making rings and bangles. They come in a variety of sizes and shapes, in both plastic and metal.

4 Emery paper

Used to soften sharp edges on findings and wire or to smooth the edge of clay pieces. Specialist foam-backed emery paper holds its shape and works really well on clay.

5 Bead knotter

This is a tool that helps to create neat-looking even knots in thread. It is especially good for working with pearls.

6 Beading needles

Fine needles are available to use with beading thread. They come in a few different sizes and are made to go through tiny seed beads with very small holes.

Materials

The projects in this book are made using materials that are easy to track down and reasonably cheap to buy.

EMBELLISHMENTS

The sky is the limit when it comes to selecting decorative materials for your jewelry-making projects. Give your imagination free rein and experiment with different types of beads, crystals, buttons, and charms.

1 Beads

There is such a large variety of beads available, from tiny seed beads to large handmade lampwork-glass beads. Beads can be made from plastic (also called Lucite), wood, metal, glass, resin, or crystal.

2 Crystals

Crystals come as beads, pendants, buttons, flat-back stones, and pointed-back stones (called chatons). They are beautiful and add sparkle to designs. Flat-back stones and chatons can be used with resin clay, or stuck on anything with the appropriate glue.

3 Buttons

Shaped buttons are great for jewelry, as they come with pre-made holes to attach them to jumprings or wire.

4 Charms

Charms can be metal, plastic, wood, or pretty much any material. The term "charm" is often applied to any jewelry item that has a hole or loop at the top to attach it to the piece.

1

2

3

4

STRINGING MATERIALS, WIRE, AND CHAIN

You have a wide of array of materials to choose from when it comes to selecting what you will use to tie your jewelry together. From rustic, natural materials like leather to strong but light nylon, stringing material can be a design feature or almost invisible.

1 Nylon-coated wire
This wire is great for stringing, as it has a better strength for heavy beads than ordinary threads. It also holds a nice shape on the neck.

2 Leather/cord/suede
These types of cords come in various colors and thicknesses. They can be knotted securely with ease or used with ribbon crimps or neck ends.

3 Beading thread
This is used with beading needles for seed beading and bead weaving. The thicker thread can be used for bead stringing and secured with necklace (calotte) ends.

4 Wire
Wire comes in a large range of sizes. It is often referred to in the United States by gauge, and United Kingdom by millimeters. It also sometimes known by Standard Wire Gauge (SWG). When starting out, buy plated wire, as it is much cheaper than precious metal. Look for a non-tarnishing variety so it doesn't discolor against your skin.

5 Chain
There are many styles of chain and a variety of colors available. Fine chains are good for hanging pendants and large-link chains are good for making charm bracelets or for adding beads to the individual links.

6 Illusion thread
This type of beading thread is clear so you cannot see it at all. It got its name from the style of necklace that has beads hanging on the thread (where there is space between the beads) creating the illusion that the beads are floating. It can be used as normal stringing thread and can be knotted and secured with glue.

7 Elastic thread
This type of thread comes in a variety of thicknesses and is great for creating designs that need to stretch over the head or hands. It can be knotted, so it is easy for children to use, as no clasps are required.

8 Memory wire
Memory wire comes in necklace and bracelet sizes. It is a very hard wire that has been created to hold its shape. You can pull it apart to thread on beads and when you let go of the wire it will reform into a circle. It is good to use for choker-style necklaces and coiled bracelets.

9 Ribbon
There are many styles and sizes of ribbon available to use with jewelry making. Whatever you choose to make you will find a fabric and color to suit your design.

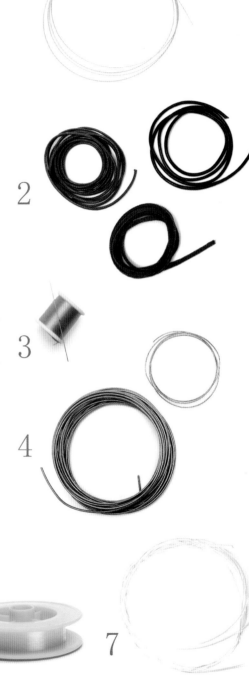

FINDINGS

Findings are all the items you use to make jewelry, which are not beads, pendants, or charms—they are all the essential little bits that hold your pieces together.

1 Jumprings

A jumpring is a single ring of wire that is used to join pieces together. They come in every size you can think of and many different colors.

2 Headpins and eyepins

These are pieces of wire with a flat or ball end (headpin) or a loop at the end (eyepin). Thread a bead on the wire and make a loop at the open end to secure the bead in place. Eyepins can be linked together to make a chain.

3 Earwires

Earwires come in various styles, from a simple "U" shape with a loop, to ones with a bead and coil finish. The loop is opened to thread on the earring piece.

4 Post and back

Posts come with a bead and open loop or with a blank disc front. The disc style is used with glue. They are often supplied with butterfly or scroll backs.

5 Clasps

There are many different types of clasp available, including slides, bolts, triggers, and even magnetic varieties. Choose a clasp to suit your design and also consider who will be wearing the piece.

A TRIGGER

Also known as a lobster or parrot clasp. These are the most widely used clasps on the market. Some come with a jumpring attached and they vary in size and style.

B BOLT RING

Similar to the trigger clasp, and used in exactly the same way, the spring-closing mechanism pushes a bar across the opening.

C MAGNETIC

These are great for bracelets when making them for yourself or for any person who finds opening and closing clasps difficult. Keep in mind that magnets will attach to some base metals, such as plated chains.

D PUSH BUTTON

These clasps have a ball on one piece and a ring on the other. Both sides have loops to attach to necklaces. The ball pushes through the ring and holds closed, as it is slightly larger than the hole in the ring.

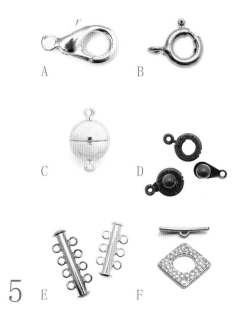

E SLIDE

This type of clasp has a barrel and loops on either side of the barrel. It is available with anything from one loop to five loops on either side. The barrel comes in two parts with one sliding into the other. Often the barrel has a magnet at the bottom to help it stay closed.

F TOGGLE

A great choice when making the clasp a feature in your design, a toggle has a loop on one end and a bar that fits through the loop to attach to the other end.

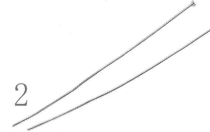

1 Ribbon crimp and cord ends

This is used to secure cord or ribbon. Ribbon crimps hinge from the top to trap the ribbon. Necklace or cord ends have side flaps that fold over the cord.

2 Bead caps

These are slightly domed shapes with a hole in the center and fit over the ends of beads as extra decoration.

3 Hair clip

These clips are usually made from metal and can be pushed open and then spring closed to grasp the hair. They are great for gluing things onto for simple hair accessories.

4 Brooch back/bar

This is a brooch pin on a bar that has holes to attach it to the piece being made as a brooch. It can be sewn on, attached with wire, or glued.

5 Blanks

These are pieces with a plate fixed to the top that you can glue decoration to. You can get blanks on ring shanks, cufflinks, and as buttons.

6 Bezel blanks

These are flat plates with a shallow wall around the sides, either with a loop on one end to attach to a chain or attached to cufflink backs, ring shanks, or bracelets. They can be filled with resin or clay. They come in a variety of shapes.

7 Sieves

These are shallow domes of metal with holes that you can attach decorations to. Sieves come as rings, brooches, or plain to attach to jumprings. They often come with a domed backing plate with small hinges to attach the sieve.

8 Crimp beads and tubes

Crimp beads look like small metal beads with large holes or tubes. They work by compressing stringing materials together to hold them in place. This technique is used to keep beads in place on a thread or on the end of a string of beads to create a loop in a thread to attach a jumpring or clasp (see page 21). They are at their best when used with crimping pliers, as they make a nice barrel crimp but they can also be simply squashed flat with flat-nose pliers as well.

9 Crimp covers

Used with crimp beads, these cover the crimp to make it look like a normal small bead. They come in a variety of metal color finishes.

10 Calottes

These are small-hinged cups with a loop on one cup, which can either be at the top opposite the hinge or on the side. The loop comes either open or closed: the open variety is often "U"-shaped and you use round-nose pliers to close it into a circle; the closed ones come with the loop as a jumpring attached to the edge of the cup. There is a hole in the middle of the hinge to take thread, and calottes work by holding a crimp inside the cup with the thread exiting through the hole in the hinge. A clasp is attached to the loop and the beads strung on the thread. Another calotte is used at the other end to finish the piece.

11 Filigree shapes

Filigree is the term used for lace-like open design on metal shapes. These shapes are available in a wide variety of styles and come in many metal colors.

12 Watch faces

Watch faces for jewelry making come with either one or two loops on the sides to attach them to thread for the strap.

13 Wire guardians

These are used to protect your thread from wearing against clasps or jumprings. Thread sits in a groove on the outside of the wire guardian, so the guardian sits against the jumpring or clasp. They make a nice neat finish to jewelry pieces as well.

Techniques

The following pages will illustrate some of the basic techniques needed to make your own jewelry and complete the projects in this book.

Opening and closing a jumpring

To make sure that jumprings shut securely, it is important to know how to open and close them correctly. You will need two pairs of pliers with flat jaws—chain-nose or flat-nose pliers will work.

1   Take a jumpring with the opening centered at the top and hold in two pairs of pliers. Holding the jumpring this way—with one pair of pliers across one side of the ring—helps to stabilize large rings.

2   You can also hold the pliers this way, with both pairs facing inward. Both ways are fine, and the way you need to attach the jumpring often dictates how you hold it.

3   Hold the jumpring on both sides and twist one hand toward you and the other hand away. This will keep the ring round in shape. Reverse the action to close the ring. Don't ever pull the ring apart as that will warp the shape. Use this technique to open loops on eyepins too.

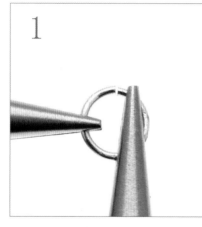

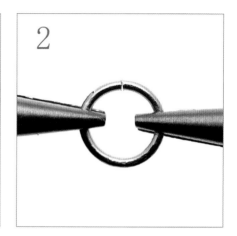

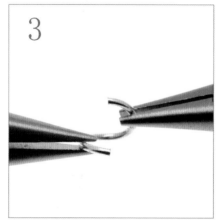

If you find your pliers mark the jumprings, wrap a bit of masking tape around the ends.

Making jumprings

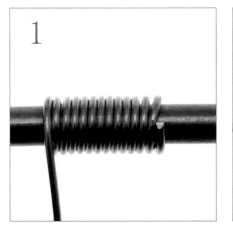

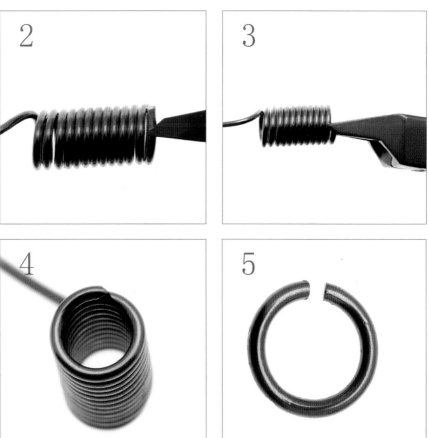

If you use a lot of jumprings and want them in different sizes, it is very easy to make your own with spare ends of wire.

1 Using a rod that is the right diameter for the jumprings you want, such as a knitting needle, wind your wire around the rod to make a coil. For most projects, US 20-gauge (SWG 21, 0.8mm) wire will work well for rings under 8mm. Use larger wire for bigger jumprings. Keep the coil as tight as you can.

2 Take a pair of side cutters—if you can get semi-flush cutters they will give you the best result—and with the flat side facing the coil, snip off the very end.

3 Now turn the cutters around so that the flat side faces away from the main coil and snip the ring off the coil. Get the pliers as close to the cut end as possible so you achieve a full circle of wire.

4 When you have cut each ring off you'll see the end looks beveled, as in this image. You need to get rid of this beveled edge to give your rings a straight edge so they close well.

5 Turn the cutters again and snip off the very end of the coil (as in Step 2), you will need to do this for each ring. This feels long-winded but it makes your jumprings look better. When cut, your rings should look like this one. To close the gap on the ring, hold it in the pliers as per the instruction on the facing page and wiggle the ring back and forth, pushing the ring gently together.

Attaching a cord end

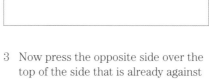

There are lots of different styles to choose from, so pick one to complement the piece you are making.

1 Take a cord end and place the end of the cord level with the end by the loop.

2 Press one side over the cord with chain-nose or flat-nose pliers.

3 Now press the opposite side over the top of the side that is already against the cord. Press the edge from the middle or it will not bend level.

4 Use the pliers to make sure the tube you have created is even and the cord end looks tidy. Finally, give the pliers a good squeeze to make sure the end is secure.

Making a wrapped loop

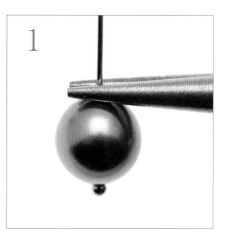

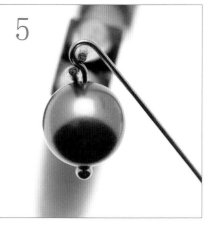

2

3

4

6

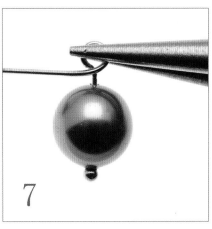

7

8

10

Loops have a multitude of functions in making jewelry, so making them properly is a skill worth mastering. This style of loop is the most secure. Once attached, it cannot be removed unless it is cut off.

1   Thread a bead onto a head or eyepin. Grip the wire with round-nose pliers next to the bead.

2   Bend the wire above the plier jaw to a right angle. You will need about ⅛in (2mm) of wire above the bead before the bend.

3   Move the plier jaws to sit at the top of the bend.

4   Use your thumb to push the wire back around the pliers, keeping it tight to the jaw.

5   Keep pushing the wire around the jaw until you meet the bead.

6   Move the pliers around the loop to hold it close to the open side and continue to bend the wire around until it is facing out at a right angle. You should now have a complete loop.

7   If adding the loop to chain or a jumpring, thread the loop onto the chain at this stage. Use a pair of chain-nose pliers to hold the loop firmly. Make sure any chain or ring is above the pliers.

8   Wrap the wire around the neck of the loop until it meets the bead.

9   Use side cutters to snip off any excess wire. Make sure the flat side of the cutter jaws is facing the coil.

10 Take the chain-nose pliers and push the cut end of the wire into the coil, so that it sits flush.

Making a simple loop

A simple, or open, loop can be opened and closed to allow it to be attached and detached as desired.

1 Thread the bead onto a head or eyepin and cut the pin about ⅜in (10mm) above the bead.

2 Bend the wire to a right angle above the bead.

3 Using round-nose pliers, grasp the wire at the very end and curl it around the plier jaws.

4 Roll the wire around to meet the bead.

5 Move the plier jaws around the loop to sit by the bead, away from the open end. Bend the loop back to sit directly about the bead.

6 Use chain-nose pliers to tighten the loop by wiggling it until the gap is closed.

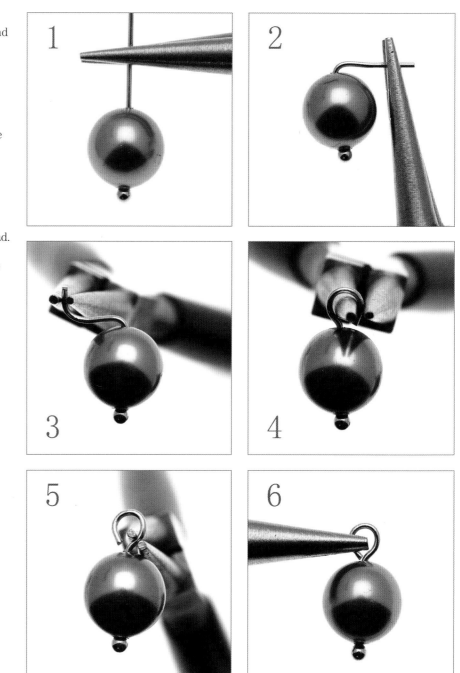

Using crimp beads

A crimp bead can be either tube-shaped or spherical—they work the same way. If crimps are done correctly they will provide a strong hold for any type of stringing material.

1 Feed the crimp onto thread and create a loop by threading the strand back through the crimp bead. Hold the crimp bead in the pliers with the bead sat in the hole that has a round side opposite a "W" shape. The crimp should be level with the edge of the plier jaws.

2 Before closing the pliers, make sure the bead is sat straight. If it's wonky then the crimp will not close correctly. Press the pliers to squash the crimp closed.

3 Move the "U"-shaped crimp to the other hole in the pliers with two round sides. Turn the crimp so the "U" faces sideways to the plier jaws.

4 Press the pliers closed tightly. This will push the sides of the "U" shape together to make a tube shape again, with the thread trapped securely.

Adding a crimp cover

To give a professional-looking finish, it's a good idea to cover crimp beads with a crimp cover.

1 Take a crimp cover and place it over the crimped bead, making sure the bead is completely inside the cover. Take a pair of chain- or flat-nose pliers and carefully grasp the cover either side of the opening.

2 Gently press the bead closed, making sure it closes completely with the sides together.

Turquoise Sea

Use gorgeous colored seed beads to create this eye-catching beach-inspired set by Sian Hamilton. The beautiful beads, in three different shades of green, are reminiscent of the sparkling sea.

FOR THE NECKLACE YOU WILL NEED

296 x 3.3mm (size 6) seed beads, matt, frosted sea green

207 x 3.3mm (size 6) seed beads, colored, sea-green-lined aqua

144 x 3.3 mm (size 6) seed beads, silver-lined jade green

1 x roll of US 22-gauge (SWG 23, 0.6mm) wire or 17 x 4in (100mm), 12 x 3in (75mm), 18 x 2in (50mm) eyepins

39⅜in (1m) x 0.5mm leather cord (add more for longer necklace)

4 x crimp beads and crimp covers

2 x jumprings and cord ends

1 x clasp

Side cutters

Chain-nose pliers

Round-nose pliers

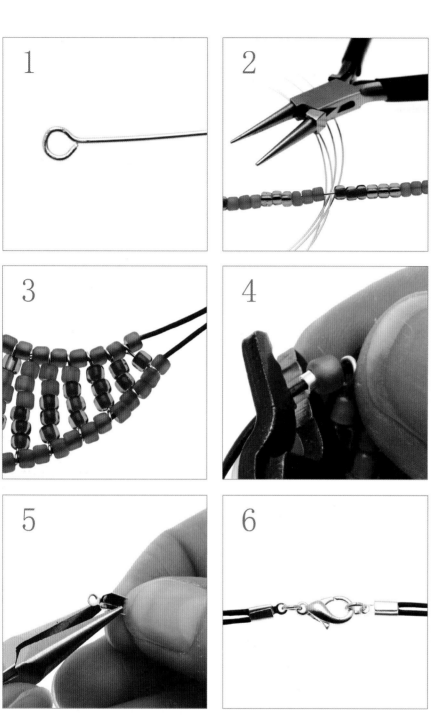

The seed beads used for the collar are quite large but this style would also suit smaller beads. Just remember you will need more beads if you use smaller ones.

Necklace

1 Take the roll of wire and thread on 24 seed beads: three colored, three matt, three silver-lined, three matt, three colored, three silver-lined, three matt, three colored. Make a loop at the end of the wire (see page 20) and cut off the roll ⅜in (10mm) from the last bead and make another loop. If using eyepins start with the 4in (100mm) ones.

2 The first step has made the middle (longest) beaded pin. Now you need to make two each of the shorter ones, removing a seed bead from the top of the stack each time—so the next two have 23 beads with only two colored at the top, not three. Use the image on page 22 as your guide. Always cut about ⅜in (10mm) from the end of the wire to give yourself enough room to make the loop. If using eyepins, as the number of beads reduces, move to shorter pins.

3 When you have finished beading the eyepins you should have 47 in total. Line them up to create the crescent shape and lay to one side. Cut two pieces of leather cord, 15¾in (400mm) and 20in (500mm), and thread a seed bead on to each cord. Thread on the first beaded pin (with one seed bead on it). Thread a seed bead on the shorter cord and two on the longer cord. Now add the next beaded pin. Continue like this until you have used all the beaded pins, always adding two beads to the longer cord (this is the outer edge).

4   To secure the crescent in place on the cord, you'll need to crimp the ends each side of the single-beaded pins. Thread a crimp onto the cord, place close to the beaded crescent, and close with either crimping or chain-nose pliers. Add a crimp cover (see page 21) to make a neat finish. Repeat this for the other three ends.

5   Measure the length you want the necklace to be and cut the cords level at this point. Take a cord end and place the two cords from one side together, level with the loop at the end. Hold them in place with your thumb and flatten one side over against the cords with chain-nose pliers. Then squash the other side over on top of the first side. Give the flattened ends a good squeeze with the pliers to make sure it is secure. Repeat for the other side.

6   Finally, take a jumpring and attach to the loop on one of the cord ends (see page 18). Use another jumpring to attach a clasp to the other end. This necklace was made choker style, as it sits well at this length.

Bracelet

YOU WILL NEED

215 x 3.3mm (size 6) seed beads, matt, frosted sea green

129 x 3.3mm (size 6) seed beads, colored, sea-green-lined aqua

129 x 3.3 mm (size 6) seed beads, silver-lined jade green

1 x roll bracelet-sized memory wire

43 x 2in (50mm) eyepins

4 x 5mm jumprings

2 x magnetic clasps

Memory-wire cutters

Make up 43 identical beaded eyepins, using the same technique as in the main steps. Cut two complete loops from the bracelet memory wire and thread the beaded eyepins onto the memory wire, adding beads in between. Make a loop at either end of the memory wire and add a magnetic clasp to each wire loop with the jumprings.

Earrings

YOU WILL NEED

32 x 3.3mm (size 6) seed beads, matt, frosted sea green

26 x 3.3mm (size 6) seed beads, colored, sea-green-lined aqua

20 x 3.3 mm (size 6) seed beads, silver-lined jade green

1 x roll of US 22-gauge (SWG 23, 0.6mm) wire or 6 x 2in (50mm) eyepins

10 x 2in (50mm) headpins

2 x earwires

2 x 10mm jumprings

Make a set of five beaded headpins. Refer to the image for the bead order. The shortest pin has five beads on it. Add one more bead to each pin. Make simple loops at the top of each headpin (see page 20) and thread onto an eyepin, adding beads in between, and make another simple loop at the end of the eyepin. Make two more plain eyepins to the same length as the beaded eyepin. Attach these to the ends of the beaded eyepin and thread the free ends onto a 10mm jumpring. Add an earwire before closing the jumpring.

Fire & Ice

A mixture of fiery crystals and silver make a stunning contrast of colors and textures in these designs by Helen Sadler.

FOR THE EARRINGS YOU WILL NEED

59in (1.5m) of US 22-gauge (SWG 23, 0.6mm) silver-plated wire

2 x hammered extra-large ring pendants, antique silver

2 x hammered circle pendants, antique silver

2 x French earwires, antique silver

8 x 4.5mm jumprings, antique silver

2 x 6mm jumprings, antique silver

6 x 1in (25mm) headpins, antique silver

18 x 4mm bicone crystals, Indian pink

18 x 4mm bicone crystals, topaz

18 x 4mm bicone crystals, ruby

Side cutters

Round-nose pliers

Keep an even spacing between the crystals when wrapping. Keep the wrapping tight to stop the crystals moving around.

Earrings

1 Use cutters to cut an approx. 30in (750mm) length of wire. Start by wrapping the end of the wire tightly around the large ring near the hole. Make several tight wraps close together to anchor it in place.

2 To add the crystals, take the wire under the ring threading on a bead and then wrap over the top. Add the crystals in an alternating pattern, leaving around 3/16in (5mm) between each wrap. You should fit 21 beads on to the ring.

3 Secure the wrapping in the same way as you started in step 1 and trim the excess. Open a 6mm jumpring (see page 16) and thread in through the top hole of the ring and then close it. Using a 4.5mm jumpring, attach the French earwire.

4 To make the dangles, thread two of each color crystal onto separate headpins. Use round-nose pliers to make a wrapped loop on each (see page 18). Thread all three dangles onto a 4.5mm jumpring.

5 Open a 4.5mm jumpring and thread it through the hole in the small hammered disc. Attach the jumpring, holding the dangles and close.

6 Use a 4.5mm jumpring to attach the disc holding the dangles to the larger jumpring on the large hammered ring. Ensure that both the hammered ring and the disc are facing the same way, hammered side forward.

Keyring

YOU WILL NEED

1 x handbag charm clip

1 x circle pendant, antique silver

1 x etched jumpring

2 x 4.5mm jumprings, antique silver

9 x 6mm jumprings, antique silver

5 x 1in (25mm) headpins, antique silver

1 x 5mm bicone crystals, topaz

3 x 4mm bicone crystals, Indian pink

3 x 4mm bicone crystals, ruby

3 x 4mm bicone crystals, topaz

To make the keyring repeat Steps 4 and 5. Make a chain of seven 6mm jumprings using one more 6mm jumpring to attach the etched jumpring. Use wrapped loops to add dangles. Use a 6mm jumpring to join the disc and chain links to the bag clip.

Play with different combinations of exotic colors. Try combining deep purple with bright blue and topaz!

Ring

YOU WILL NEED

1 x 9-loop bling ring silver-plated

28 x 1in (25mm) headpins, antique silver

35 x 4–8mm bicone beads in topaz, Indian pink, and ruby

For a fabulously sparkly ring thread one or two crystals on to a headpin and attach them to a bling ring base with a simple loop technique (see page 20). Continue until you have used all the headpins or there is no more space.

Perfect Plaits

Make this unique plaited jewelry set by Gemma Reilly, which brings together a variety of textures. The muted tones of suede and wood create a lovely touch when worn with a bright dress.

FOR THE NECKLACE YOU WILL NEED

54 x 8mm natural wooden beads

10 x 5mm opaque, round lampwork beads, sunny yellow

6 x cord ends, silver-plated

1 x trigger clasp, silver-plated

1 x extension chain, silver-plated

10 x 1in (25mm) headpins, silver-plated

39⅜in (1m) waxed cord, natural

39⅜in (1m) heavy chain, silver-plated

79in (2m) fake suede, yellow

8 x 5mm jumprings, silver-plated

2 x decorative spacers, silver-plated

Scissors

Round-nose pliers

Chain-nose pliers

Side cutters

Necklace

1 Fold each side of a cord end in slightly. Place the end of the waxed cord into the cord end and with the chain-nose pliers squeeze it flat. Thread on 54 wooden beads and add a second cord end so that the beads are held tightly in place. Trim the excess cord.

2 Cut the suede in half and add a cord end to one end of each length of suede.

3 Use 5mm jumprings to add the chain, the beaded cord, and the two pieces of suede to each loop on the decorative spacer (see page 16).

4 Attach the spacer to something sturdy and plait tightly along the whole length. Trim the excess chain and suede. Add a cord end to each end of the suede.

5 Attach a second decorative spacer to hold everything in place. Use a 5mm jumpring to attach a trigger to one side and another to add an extension chain to the other.

6 Thread a yellow bead onto a headpin, trim ⅜in (10mm) above the bead, bend the pin into a loop, and attach it to the chain. Close the loop. Only add the beaded headpins to one side of the necklace, with two per section. Work out from the center to create a symmetrical piece. Add ten in total.

For an opulent version of this necklace. Swap the wooden beads for pearls.

Bracelet

YOU WILL NEED

24 x 8mm natural wooden beads

14 x 5mm opaque, round lampwork beads, sunny yellow

6 x cord ends, silver-plated

1 x trigger clasp, silver-plated

14 x 1in (25mm) headpins, silver-plated

20in (0.5m) waxed cord, natural

20in (0.5m) heavy chain, silver-plated

39⅜in (1m) fake suede, yellow

2 x 8mm jumprings, silver-plated

Thread 24 wooden beads onto the waxed cord. Add the leather crimps in the same way. Follow the steps for the necklace, but instead of the decorative spacers, just use 8mm jumprings. Add the yellow beads to both sides of the bracelet until you have used all 14 of them.

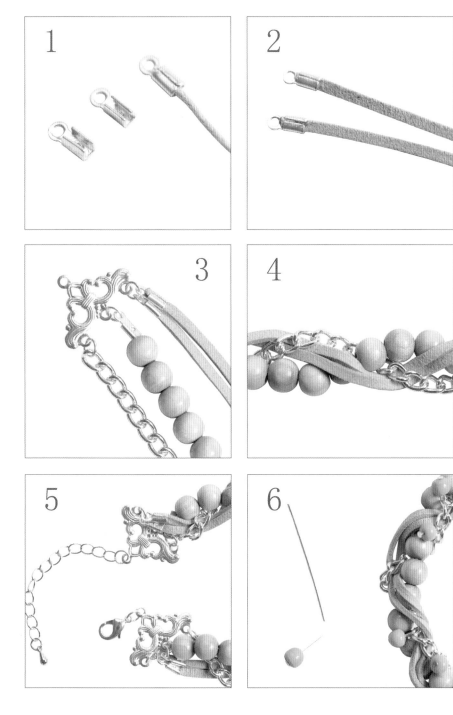

Earrings

YOU WILL NEED

6 x 8mm natural wooden beads

14 x 5mm opaque, round lampwork beads, sunny yellow

5in (120mm) heavy chain, silver-plated

2 x long earwires, silver-plated

20 x 1in (25mm) headpins, silver-plated

6 x 2.5mm (size 8) rocailles (round seed beads), silver-lined

Cut a 2½in (60mm) length of chain. Add a long earwire to one end. Thread a yellow bead onto a headpin. Trim ⅜in (10mm) above the bead, bend the pin into a loop, and attach it to the last link of the chain. Close the loop. Add six more yellow beads randomly along the chain. Add three wooden beads, but use a rocaille bead as a stopper on the headpin. Repeat the process to make a pair.

Take your time with the plaiting to make sure it is neat and even. Move the strands around before you finish the plaiting to ensure you are happy before you add the second decorative spacer.

Orbital Rays

Choose your favorite colors to create the links in this simple but spectacular chainmaille jewelry set by Sarah Austin.

FOR THE BRACELET YOU WILL NEED

9 x inner diameter 10.4mm, 1.29mm bronze jumprings (A)

52 x inner diameter 6mm, 1.02mm bronze jumprings (B)

9 x inner diameter 6.7mm, 1.02mm bronze jumprings (C)

30 x inner diameter 4.3mm, 1mm anodized aluminum jumprings, ice pink

24 x inner diameter 4.3mm, 1mm anodized aluminum jumprings, ice blue

24 x inner diameter 4.3mm, 1mm anodized aluminum jumprings, lavender

1 x copper-plated jubilee heart toggle

2 x pairs chain-nose, flat-nose, or bent-nose pliers

Bracelet

1 Link eight closed ice-blue jumprings with one large, bronze ring (A) (see page 16). Separate the ice-blue rings into two groups of four. Link two bronze rings (B) through one set of four ice-blue rings and two more bronze rings (B) through the second set of four ice-blue rings. Lay out the rings as shown.

2 Fold back the right-hand pair of rings (B) added in Step 1. Between the first two rings of this set of four, link one ice-blue ring to the folded back rings (B).

3 Between the third and fourth rings of the same set of four, link one ice-blue ring to the folded back rings (B). Repeat Steps 2–3 for the second set of four ice-blue rings.

4 Rotate the left-hand set of rings so that the rings added in Steps 2–3 are in the center of the large ring. Link one medium-sized ring (C) between the second and third ice-blue rings of the right-hand set. Do not close ring C.

5 Rotate ring C into the center of the large ring (A) and link the open ring C between the second and third ice-blue rings of the left-hand set. Close ring C. Repeat Steps 1–5 to make three components in ice blue, ice pink, and lavender.

6 Using two of the small rings (B) to link the components, either alternating the colors or joining them into color blocks. Link two closed ice-pink rings to one end of the bracelet using two ice-pink rings. Connect the toggle bar to the last pair of ice-pink rings just added, using one ice-pink ring. Attach the toggle ring to the other end of the bracelet using one ice-pink ring.

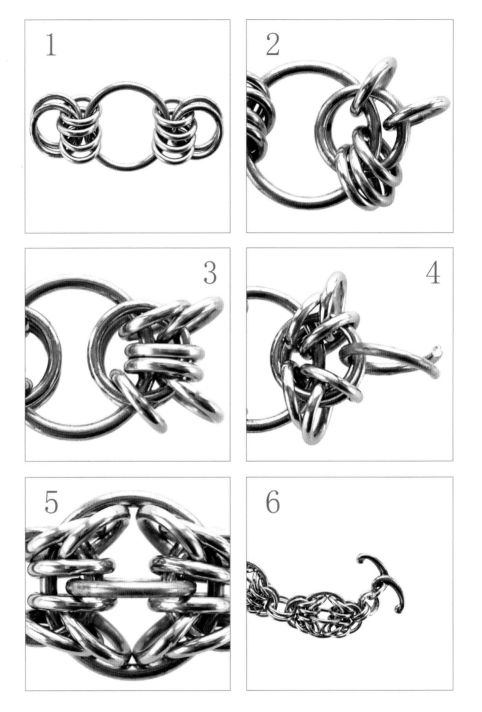

Try using brass instead of bronze, and jewel-like colors such as red, royal blue, and green.

Necklace

YOU WILL NEED

9 x inner diameter 10.4mm, 1.29mm bronze jumprings (A)

52 x inner diameter 6mm, 1.02mm bronze jumprings (B)

9 x inner diameter 6.7mm, 1.02mm bronze jumprings (C)

36 x inner diameter 4.3mm, 1mm anodized aluminum jumprings, ice pink

36 x inner diameter 4.3mm, 1mm anodized aluminum jumprings, ice blue

36 x inner diameter 4.3mm, 1mm anodized aluminum jumprings, lavender

1 x copper-plated jubilee heart toggle

Make three components in each color following Steps 1–5 of the main project. Link the components together in sets, one of each color in each set. Take one set and attach the other two to one end using two medium-sized closed rings (B) per set (so it looks like the letter Y). Make a chain by joining two medium-sized closed rings (B) with two colored rings until your necklace is a length you like (the material jumpring quantity makes a 16in/405mm chain). Attach the chain to the Y shape with sets of two colored rings. If the chain is made long enough to go over your head you do not need a clasp. If making a shorter chain, find the middle of the chain and open a jumpring at that point. Add a toggle clasp with the bar on one end of the chain and the loop on the other.

Earrings

YOU WILL NEED

2 x inner diameter 10.4mm, 1.29mm bronze jumprings (A)

8 x inner diameter 6mm, 1.02mm bronze jumprings (B)

2 x inner diameter 6.7mm, 1.02mm bronze jumprings (C)

12 x inner diameter 4.3mm, 1mm anodized aluminum jumprings, ice pink

8 x inner diameter 4.3mm, 1mm anodized aluminum jumprings, ice blue

8 x inner diameter 4.3mm, 1mm anodized aluminum jumprings, lavender

2 x 6mm bicone, rose colored

2 x 6mm bicone, violet colored

2 x 6mm bicone, aquamarine colored

2 x 1in (25mm) bronze eyepins

2 x 1in (25mm) bronze headpins

2 x earwires, bronze

Make two components with these changes to the main project steps:
Step 1. Each set of four rings is made up of two ice-blue rings with one lavender ring on either side.
Steps 2 and 3. Use ice-pink rings. Link one ice-pink ring to the end of each completed component.
Attach one 6mm rose bicone on an eyepin to the earwire and ice-pink ring, making a simple loop (see page 20) on the open end. Thread one 6mm aquamarine and violet bicone on a headpin, make a simple loop at the end and add to the other ice-pink ring.

Break up lengths of chain with components and matching beads.

Persian Memories

Make these beautiful Persian-inspired designs by Jessica Rose, combining onyx faceted drops with a rich, golden chain and fuchsia-dyed agate. Black onyx contrasted with bright agate and gold gives a luxurious feel to these pieces.

FOR THE NECKLACE YOU WILL NEED

1 x strand of large faceted onyx drops

1 x strand of 8mm, round micro-faceted fuchsia or purple agate

10 x 4mm, matte metallic gold multi-faceted round fire-polished glass beads

1 x roll of tigertail wire

3 x different-sized gold-plated chains, approx. 20in (500mm) of each

1 x roll of US 18-gauge (SWG 19, 1mm) gold-plated wire

4 x small gold-plated crimps

1 x medium-sized gold-plated lobster clasp

4 x 6mm gold-plated jumprings

Chain-nose pliers

Round-nose pliers

Side cutters

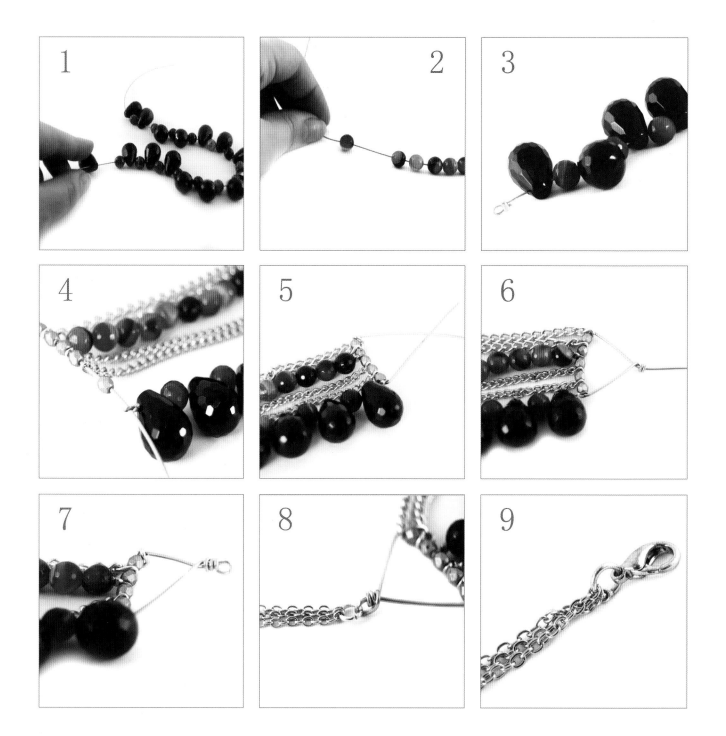

Necklace

1 Cut a piece of tigertail approx. 20in (500mm) long. Thread your beads onto the strand, alternating the black onyx drops with the round pink agate until it has reached the desired length for the front of your necklace. This should be around 10–11¾in (250–300mm) long.

2 Repeat the process with a second strand of tigertail, this time using just the round pink agate beads. For a slightly different look you could use different colored beads—the most important thing to maintain the style of the necklace is the shape of the beads, so choose round and drop-shaped ones.

3 Crimp both ends of each strand individually to secure the beads in place, using a total of four small, gold-plated crimp beads (see page 21). Be sure to leave a small loop, big enough to fit the US 18-gauge wire through at each crimped end. Also, allow the beads a bit of breathing space, as they will be curved when on the neck. Finally, make sure the strand containing only the round beads is slightly shorter than the other, as it will be placed higher up on the necklace.

4 Cut four strands of gold-plated chain, using two slightly different types. They will need to be roughly the same size, as the beaded strands, but make them slightly larger at this stage—you can cut them down later. Thread the chain and beaded wires onto a piece of the gold-plated wire, using the small golden beads to create a space between each strand.

5 Using chain-nose pliers, bend each end of the wire to create a triangular shape where the two ends cross at the top. Once you have done this on one side, thread all the strands and chain onto a new piece of gold-plated wire, placing small gold beads in between as spacers. At this stage you will need to do some measuring by eye and cut the gold-plated chain down so that all the wires and chains sit nicely.

6 Wrap one end of the gold-plated wire around the other 2–3 times and cut the end off with your side cutters. Be sure to tuck the sharp end in with your chain-nose pliers to finish and leave the remaining longer end of wire out straight in front, ready to make a loop with (see page 18).

7 Using round-nose pliers, create a secure loop with the remaining piece of wire. Be sure to wrap the end around the base of the loop a few times before cutting and tucking the wire end in as before. Repeat Steps 6 and 7 on the other end so that it is symmetrical.

8 Using a gold-plated jumpring, attach three strands of gold-plated chain to the loop at one end of the necklace—the chain strands will need to be around 6in (150mm) long, depending on where you want the necklace to sit. Hold it up to your neck to test the length before cutting them. Repeat the same process on the other side of the necklace.

9 At either end of the necklace, join the three chains together using a gold-plated jumpring. On one side attach your gold-plated lobster clasp and on the other side attach a short piece of thicker gold-plated chain to provide an adjustable length. Ensure that the chain is thin enough to fit in the clasp.

Earrings

YOU WILL NEED

2 x large faceted onyx drops

8 x 8mm, round micro-faceted fuchsia or purple agate

28 x 4mm, matte metallic gold multi-faceted round fire-polished glass beads

1 x roll of tigertail wire

4 x small gold-plated crimps

2 x gold-plated earwires

2 x 6mm gold-plated jumprings

You can make a matching pair of earrings using tigertail. Simply thread your beads on with a black onyx drop bead in the center, as shown in the picture. Make a loop on each end of the tigertail following Step 3 of the main project. Crimp the ends to secure and attach to earwires using gold-plated jumprings.

Gorgeous Glass

Faceted glass nuggets and twists are combined with colored wire to make this beautiful collection by Gemma Reilly. Add glamour to a party dress by making the set in a perfectly coordinating color.

FOR THE NECKLACE YOU WILL NEED

6 x glass nuggets, royal blue

7 x light twists, royal blue

2 x 8mm pressed round beads, royal blue

18 x crimps, silver-plated

18 x crimp covers, silver-plated

8 x crimp tubes, silver-plated

2 x 8mm jumprings, silver-plated

1 x 33ft (10m) length of plastic-coated wire, royal blue

1 x trigger clasp, silver-plated

Chain-nose pliers

Round-nose pliers

Side cutters

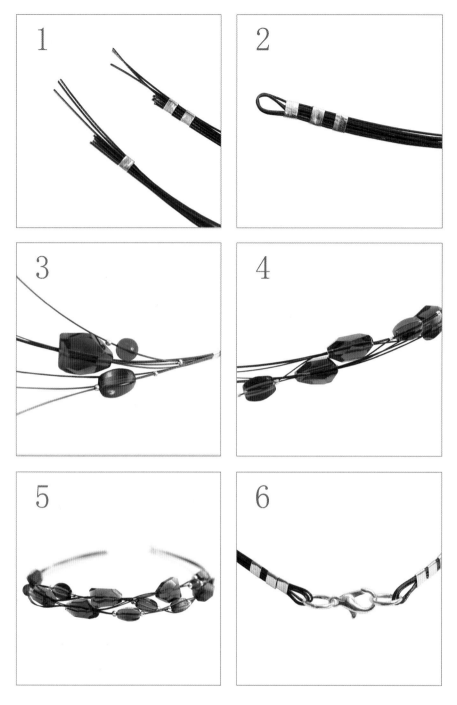

Necklace

1   Measure and cut eight 23⅝in (600mm) lengths of plastic-coated wire. Thread on a crimp tube. Move it along so it sits 1³⁄₁₆in (30mm) from the end of the wire. Squeeze the crimp flat. Trim five lengths so they are ⅜in (10mm) above the crimp. Add a second crimp, move it close to the first, and squeeze it flat.

2   Add a third crimp, and move it so it sits over the shorter lengths. Bend the longer lengths around and back into the crimp tube. Make sure they are in as far as they can go and squeeze the crimp flat.

3   Thread on another crimp tube and squeeze flat approx. 2¾in (70mm) from the first set of crimps. Start threading on the beads. You need a single strand for the round beads with a crimp on either side, two strands for the twist with a crimp on either side, and four strands for the nugget. You don't need crimps for these.

4   Use six nuggets, seven twists, and two round beads as shown. Use different strands to thread on the beads to create the desired effect. Don't crimp yet.

5   Move all of the beads around until you are happy with the layout and crimp them into place. Add a crimp cover over each crimp for a professional finish (see page 21).

6   Thread on a crimp tube to all of the strands and squeeze them flat. Add the next three crimp tubes as in Steps 1 and 2. Add a jumpring with a trigger clasp to one end and a jumpring to the other.

Bracelet

YOU WILL NEED

4 x glass nuggets, royal blue

4 x light twists, royal blue

4 x 8mm pressed round beads, royal blue

16 x crimps, silver-plated

16 x crimp covers, silver-plated

8 x crimp tubes, silver-plated

2 x 8mm jumprings, silver-plated

1 x 33ft (10m) length of plastic-coated wire, royal blue

1 x trigger clasp, silver-plated

Make the bracelet in the same way as the necklace but use 6in (150mm) lengths of plastic-coated wire.

Earrings

YOU WILL NEED

2 x 8mm pressed round beads, royal blue

2 x headpins with balls, silver-plated

2 x stud and hooks silver-plated

Thread a round bead onto a headpin. Trim ⅜in (10mm) above the bead, bend into a loop, and attach to the loop of a stud and hook. Close the loop. Repeat to make a pair.

Deco Style

Take inspiration from the 1920s Art Deco era with a crystal keystone bead jewelry set by Sian Hamilton. These beautiful beads are very flexible for use in jewelry designs.

FOR THE NECKLACE YOU WILL NEED

75 x 4mm bicone crystals, black diamond

45 x 6mm potato pearls, emerald green

8 x 17mm keystone beads, black

1 x roll of US 22-gauge (SWG 23, 0.6mm) black wire

2 x crimp beads

6 x 5mm jumprings

1 x black clasp

1 x roll of medium curb chain

1 x roll of beading thread

Beading needle

Round-nose pliers

Chain-nose pliers

Side cutters

Scissors

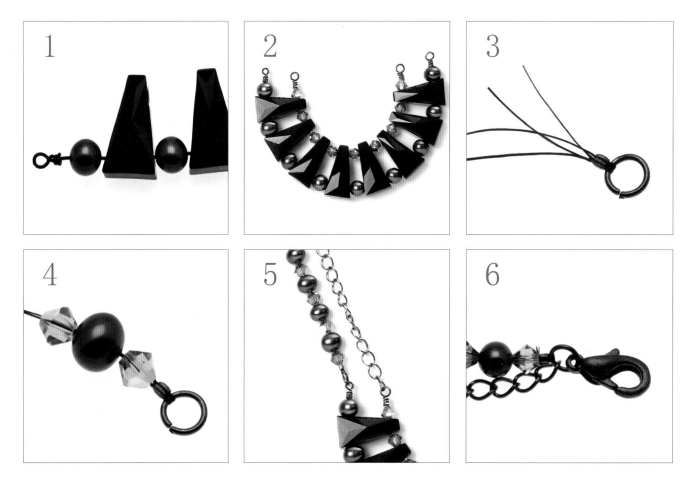

Necklace

1 To make the arch, take a 10in (250mm) length of black wire. Make a wrapped loop in one end as shown (see page 18). Thread on a pearl, then the wide end of a keystone bead. Repeat until you have nine pearls and eight keystones on the wire. Place a piece of masking tape at the open end of the wire, as you don't want to close it with a loop yet.

2 Repeat Step 1 with the inside arch of crystals in between the keystones. When you get to the end of this piece, pull all the beads tight. You will see that this naturally makes the arch shape. Create a wrapped loop, keeping it as tight as possible without damaging the beads. Now finish the outer pearl length with a wrapped loop, again pulling it tight to form the arch.

3 Take a length of beading thread and feed it onto a needle. Double up the thread and feed on a crimp bead and a closed jumpring. Take the needle back through the crimp bead, trapping the jumpring. Pull the thread tight to the ring, leaving a small tail of thread and close the crimp with crimping pliers (see page 21).

4 Cut off the tail of the thread. Starting with a crystal, feed on alternate crystals and pearls for the first nine sections, then thread on two crystals and one pearl for the next four sections, then four sections of three crystals and one pearl, with one final section of four crystals and one pearl. You will need to make two pieces, one for either side of the necklace. Repeat Step 3 to add a crimp to the ends.

5 Take one of the beaded lengths and open the jumpring (see page 16). Attach the jumpring to the outer loop on the arched keystone section. Take a length of chain and another jumpring, and attach to the inner loop on the arch section. Repeat this for the other side. Now add jumprings to pull the chains together as in the main image (see page 46), or leave it open.

6 To finish the necklace, open the jumprings at the ends of the beaded lengths. On one side attach the end of the chain and close the ring. On the other add a clasp and the chain end and close the ring.

Beading thread was used for this project, as the pearls had a very small hole. If your pearls or beads have a larger hole, you can use thicker thread on its own with no need for a needle.

Earrings

YOU WILL NEED

8 x 4mm bicone crystals, black diamond

8 x 6mm potato pearls, emerald green

6 x 17mm keystone beads, black

1 x roll of US 24-gauge (SWG 25, 0.5mm) black wire

2 x 5mm jumprings

2 x black earwires

4in (100mm) medium curb chain

Make a small spiral at the end of the colored wire, feed on pearls and keystones, and finish with another spiral. Make the crystal section the same way as the main project steps. Bend the wrapped loops upward and attach a chain with 5mm jumprings. Hang from earwires.

Bracelet

YOU WILL NEED

34 x 4mm bicone crystals, black diamond

18 x 6mm potato pearls, emerald green

8 x 17mm keystone beads, black

1 x roll of US 24-gauge (SWG 25, 0.5mm) black wire

2 x 5mm jumprings

1 x black magnetic clasp

Take two lengths of wire and make wrapped loops at one end. Feed on crystals, pearls, and the keystones. Make sure to alternate the way the keystones sit to keep the design level all the way around. Mix up the beads in whatever way you like. Finish the ends with wrapped loops and attach a 5mm jumpring through both wrapped loops on each end. Add a magnetic clasp to finish.

Filmstar Filigree

Evoke the glamour of Hollywood in the 1940s with these gorgeous makes by Janine McGinnies. Antique brass contrasts with deep red crystals to give a Gothic edge.

FOR THE EARRINGS YOU WILL NEED

2 x natural brass, 50 x 28mm deco diamond filigree

2 x natural brass, 20 x 10mm French earwires

1 x 8in (200mm) length of ⅛in (2mm) fine curb chain, antique brass

2 x 10mm bicone crystals, Siam red

2 x 11 x 5.5mm faceted drop crystals, Siam red

20 x 4mm bicone crystals, Siam red

2 x 4mm bicone crystals, erinite

2 x 9mm antique brass jumprings

2 x 5mm antique brass jumprings

8 x 4mm antique brass jumprings

1 x 39⅜in (1m) length of US 26-gauge (SWG 27, 0.4mm) antique brass craft wire

1 x antique brass eyepin

Side cutters

Chain-nose pliers

Flat-nose pliers

Earrings

1 Start by making the main part of your earring. Take one of the filigree pieces and bend it in half using a pencil. The filigree shouldn't touch at the sides—there should be a gap of about ³⁄₁₆in (5mm)—so don't squeeze it together. You can perfect the shape using a pair of chain-nose pliers.

2 Take about 20in (500mm) of craft wire and start by wrapping the wire around one side of the top hole of the filigree. Do this by threading about 2in (50mm) through the gap in the filigree and up through the front. Neatly wrap this 2in (50mm) section around and through the same hole several times to secure.

3 Add a 4mm red crystal, thread through the next hole opposite, and back up with the middle of the filigree. Add another red crystal and thread through the opposite side again. Do this until you reach the bottom, and add an erinite crystal. Carry on up the other side and secure at the top in the same way. There should be five red bicone crystals on each side and one erinite crystal.

4 Add a 10mm bicone crystal to an eyepin and make a simple loop (see page 20). Add the 9mm jumpring through the folded-over end of the filigree, so it sits in the middle. Add the 10mm crystal to the jumpring by opening the eyepin a little and close again neatly.

5 At the pointed end of the filigree, add about four links of chain to each pointed side of the filigree using 4mm jumprings. Add a 5mm jumpring to the red drop crystal and add both the ends of chain.

6 Cut two lengths of chain—around 12 links, but if your loops are bigger you may need more. Using 4mm jumprings, add a length of chain to each side of the filigree. Open the top loop of the eyepin, add on each side of the chain and the earwire in the middle. Close the eyepin and repeat the process for the other earring.

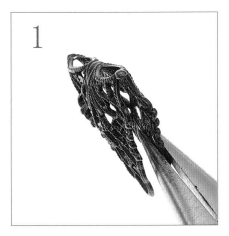

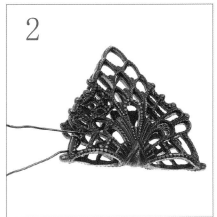

When adding the 4mm bicone crystals, remember that there are no definite, evenly spaced holes on the filigree, so you will have to thread through the next available space. It won't look perfectly even, but that is the effect.

You could buff the metal with a metal reliefing block if you wanted to achieve a more "golden" effect to the metal.

4

5

Ring

YOU WILL NEED

1 x natural brass, 50 x 28mm deco diamond filigree

6 x 11 x 5.5mm faceted drop crystals, Siam red

2 x 4mm bicone crystals, erinite

1 x 9mm antique brass jumprings

8 x 5mm antique brass jumprings

2 x 1in (25mm) antique brass headpins

Bend the filigree around a ring mandrel and perfect the shape with chain-nose pliers. It may help to flatten the filigree a little. Thread the erinite crystals onto headpins and make simple loops at the ends (see page 20). Add a 9mm jumpring to the same point as you did on the earrings and attach the erinite bicones and red drop crystals to the 9mm jumpring using 5mm jumprings.

6

Necklace

YOU WILL NEED

1 x natural brass, 50 x 28mm deco diamond filigree

1 x 20in (510mm) length of ⅛in (2mm) fine curb chain, antique brass

2 x 11 x 5.5mm faceted drop crystals, Siam red

2 x 5mm antique brass jumprings

Using one of the filigrees, bend the corners in and around to form a loop and thread your chain down this loop. Secure the chain with a red drop crystal on each side.

Peacock Feathers

Use peacock feathers to make this statement set of projects by Tansy Wilson. Show off some of nature's most stunning jewel-like colors, which have influence and symbolism in many cultures.

FOR THE NECKLACE YOU WILL NEED

1 x length of 31.5in (800mm) large-link chain, gold

5 x cord ends, gold

1 x large bolt ring, gold

5 x peacock feathers

1 x 5g bag of size 8 bronze color seed beads

1 x 5g bag of 5mm gold metal tube beads

7 x 8mm twisted jumprings, gold

4 x peacock-patterned 1³⁄₁₆in (30mm) diamond-shaped bead frames

8 x 3mm round beads, gold

8 x 50mm headpins, gold

Fine beading needle

Glue

Scissors

Side cutters

Flat-nose pliers

Keep threading the seed and tube beads onto the barbs of at least half of the feather before moving them into their final position and gluing. This is easier than gluing each strand individually.

Necklace

1 Take the large-link chain and ensure you have the same link shape at each end. At one end, attach the large bolt ring and attach the bolt ring catch at the other, using a twisted jumpring for each (see page 16).

2 Lay the chain flat on the table with the clasp joined at the top. Cut the square link that is around 6⁵⁄₁₆in (160mm) down from the top on both sides of the chain and also the square link that is around 11¾in (300mm) down from the top. Leave the links there for the time being.

3 Add a 3mm gold bead onto a headpin and thread through the peacock square bead frame, making a small loop (see page 18) as close to the other side of the bead frame as possible. Keep the excess wire on the headpin. Repeat this for the other hole on the bead frame. Do this so you have four peacock bead frames.

4 Remove the first cut link, made in Step 2, on one side of your necklace. Thread the long excess wire of the headpin through the joining loop on the actual chain so it fits snugly into the eyeloop you made in Step 3. Then wrap the long end of wire around itself, securing the bead frame in place. Cut away the excess headpin. Repeat this step, attaching the other end of the bead frame to the necklace. Repeat the whole step again to attach the other three bead frames.

5 Take five evenly sized peacock feathers and, holding one by the central quill, pull the barbs downward to strip any excess away leaving just the eye detail. Do this to all five feathers. Then starting with one feather, thread three barbs through the collapsible eye on your beading needle.

6 Thread onto the needle: one bronze seed bead followed by a gold tube bead, followed by another bronze seed bead. Pull the beading needle very gently so the beads are left threaded onto the barbs.

7 Move methodically along the feather, always catching three barbs and threading the same combination of beads as in Step 6. When you are about halfway round you can arrange the beads so they form an even curve matching that of the feather pattern. Add a drop of glue to secure them in place. When dry, continue to bead the rest of the feather and again glue to secure. Repeat Steps 6 and 7 so you have beaded all five feathers.

8 Attach a small gold cord end onto the quill of each beaded feather by squashing it on with flat-nose pliers. Make sure you have the loop facing so the feather will hang upside down when attached. Add a drop of glue to secure and cut away the excess quill. Repeat this for all five feathers.

9 Thread a jumpring through the loop on the ribbon crimp. Then thread it through the bottom wrapped eyeloop you made on the bead frame, joined to the necklace, and close. Repeat this for three more of the feathers. Finally thread a jumpring through the loop on the ribbon crimp and link the last feather to the center bottom link on the necklace and close.

Earrings
YOU WILL NEED

2 x earwires, gold

2 x 18mm disc beads, peacock

2 x 3mm round beads, gold

2 x headpins, gold

2 x 8mm twisted jumprings, gold

Thread a small gold bead onto a headpin. Thread through the peacock disc bead and make a simple eyeloop as close to the top of the disc bead as possible. Link the bead onto a gold earring hook using another twisted jumpring. Repeat for the other earring.

Bracelet
YOU WILL NEED

6 x 18mm disc beads, peacock

6 x eyepins, gold

7 x 8mm twisted jumprings, gold

1 x toggle clasp, gold

Simply thread an eyepin through each disc, making another eyeloop as close to the other side of the bead as possible. Link each bead together using a twisted jumpring for extra detail. Add a toggle clasp at the end.

Fall Elegance

A fall palette is the inspiration behind this set by Gemma Reilly. Try different color combinations to reflect the changing seasons.

FOR THE NECKLACE YOU WILL NEED

50 x 4mm faceted beads, pale pink

16 x 6mm faceted moon beads, pale pink

15 x 6mm faceted moon beads, topaz

19 x 6mm faceted beads, amber

13 x 8mm faceted beads, amber

13 x 8mm faceted beads, topaz

1 x 79in (2m) length of light chain, gold-plated

1 x three-loop slide clasp, gold-plated

6 x 5mm jumprings, gold-plated

25 x 2in (50mm) headpins, gold-plated

25 x 1in (25mm) eyepins, gold-plated

Side cutters

Round-nose pliers

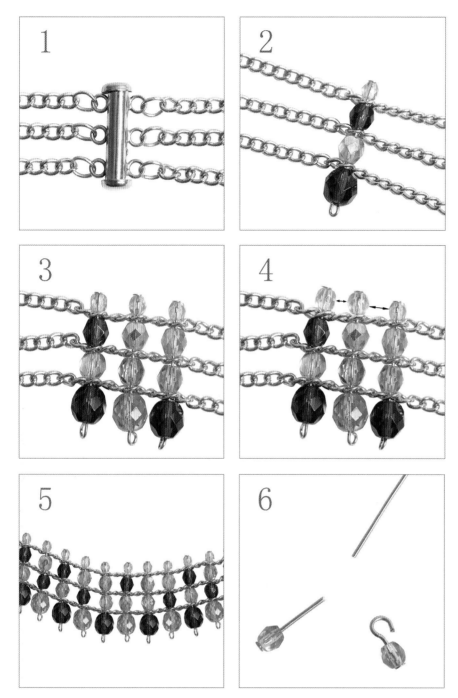

Necklace

1 Cut three lengths of chain so that you have the following links remaining in each length: 178(1), 183(2), and 190(3). Use jumprings to attach each of the chains in size order on the clasp (see page 16). Attach the second half of the clasp in the same way.

2 Thread a 4mm bead onto a headpin and pass through the 26th link of chain 1 (alternate the colors of the beads as you go), add a 6mm bead, pass through the 26th link of chain 2, add another 6mm bead, and pass through the 27th link of chain 3. Add an 8mm bead, trim the eyepin ⅜in (10mm) above the bead, and bend into a loop to close.

3 Add the second beaded headpin in the same way as in Step 2, into the third link along from the first beaded headpin. Add another headpin into the third link from the second beaded headpin.

4 Add another headpin in the same way, starting in the 54th link of chain 1, the 54th link of chain 2 and the 56th link of chain 3. Add the second beaded headpin into the second chain link along from the first beaded headpin on chain 1, but into the third links in chains 2 and 3. Add another into the third link from the second beaded headpin.

5 Add another headpin in the same way starting in the 71st link of chain 1, the 72nd link of chain 2, and the 76th link of chain 3. Continue to add headpins into every third link until you have a section of 13 headpins.

6 Add the last two beaded sections to mirror the first half of the necklace. Thread a 4mm bead onto a headpin, trim ⅜in (10mm) above the bead, and add to the bottom loop of a beaded headpin. Repeat to add one to each of the beaded headpins.

This necklace doesn't have to have one large beaded section. It would look also striking with small beaded sections all the way around it.

Earrings

YOU WILL NEED

4 x 4mm faceted beads, pale pink

2 x 8mm faceted beads, amber

2 x 8mm faceted beads, topaz

2 x 1in (25mm) headpins, gold-plated

6 x 1in (25mm) eyepins, gold-plated

2 x earwires gold-plated

Thread 4mm beads onto the headpins. Trim ⅜in (10mm) above the bead, bend into a simple loop (see page 20). Place all remaining beads on eyepins and make simple loops at the open ends. Attach the loops together to form two lengths of identical beaded chain. Add an earwire at the end of each chain.

Bracelet

YOU WILL NEED

9 x 4mm faceted beads, pale pink

9 x 6mm faceted moon beads, pale pink

9 x 6mm faceted moon beads, topaz

9 x 6mm faceted moon beads, amber

4 x 8mm faceted beads, amber

4 x 8mm faceted beads, topaz

1 x 3 loop slide clasp, gold-plated

44 x eyepins, gold-plated

Attach an eyepin to each of the loops on one side of the clasp. Add one bead to each pin, trim the eyepin ⅜in (10mm) above the bead, bend into a simple loop, add another eyepin and close the loop. Repeat to make three rows of beaded eyepins, using the beads at random. Attach the clasp to the other end of the eyepins.

Have a Heart

Create maximum impact with these eye-catching heart-shaped designs by Emma Brennan, using simple beading with wire to create several items of jewelry that really make a statement.

FOR THE EARRINGS
YOU WILL NEED

2 x 22in (550mm) lengths of US 26-gauge (SWG 27, 0.4mm) antique brass wire

20 x 8mm Lucite beads

26 x 4mm glass or Lucite beads

4 x 30mm lengths of fine chain

4 x 6mm jumprings

2 x 4mm jumprings

1 x pair of earring wires

Chain-nose pliers

Wire cutters

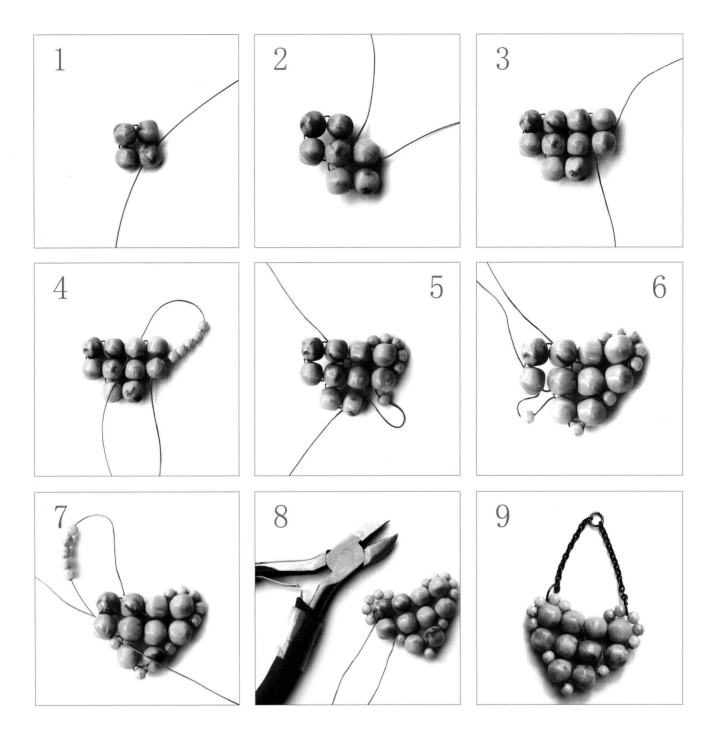

Do not overwork the wire, and try to avoid creating kinks as you work to prevent the wire from breaking.

Earrings

1 Using one wire, pick up three 8mm beads and push them to the center of the wire. Pick up a fourth 8mm bead then take both wire tails in opposite directions through the center of the bead to form a circle.

2 Pick up another two 8mm beads on the lower wire tail, then pick up a third and cross the tails of both wires in opposite directions through it.

3 On the upper wire tail, pick up another two 8mm beads, then pick up a third 8mm bead and cross both wires through it with tails exiting in opposite directions.

4 On the upward-pointing tail, thread on five 4mm beads, then take the tail through the top center right 8mm bead, and the top center left 8mm bead.

5 With the downward-pointing tail, pick up one 4mm bead and take the tail through the lower right 8mm bead.

6 Continuing with the downward pointing tail, pick up one 4mm bead and take the tail up through the lower left 8mm bead. Pick up another 4mm bead and then take the tail up through the left central 8mm bead.

7 On the upper wire tail, pick up five 4mm beads then take the tail down through the left central 8mm bead. The two wire tails should now be exiting this same bead in opposite directions.

8 Pull the wires up tight and wrap the wire tails around the supporting wires a couple of times on both sides of the bead. Clip the tails and hide them between the beads by squashing them with the tips of your pliers. Be careful not to cut the supporting wires at this point.

9 Attach a 6mm jumpring to the top of both sides of the heart, between the second and third 4mm beads on either side. While the jumpring is open, attach a 1³⁄₁₆in (30mm) length of chain to each ring. Close the ring then join both chains together with a 4mm jumpring at the top. Attach an earring wire to the jumpring to finish.

Brooch

YOU WILL NEED

1 x 22in (550mm) length of US 26-gauge (SWG 27, 0.4mm) antique brass wire

10 x 8mm Lucite beads

13 x 4mm glass/Lucite beads

2 x 1in (25mm) lengths of chain

4 x 6mm jumprings

2 x 4mm jumprings

1 x antique brass kilt pin with 3 loops

1 x antique brass heart charm

Make a single chunky heart by following the steps for the main project. Using 6mm jumprings attach the heart to the chain pieces and attach the chain to the kilt pin using 4mm jumprings. Hang the heart charm on the middle kilt-pin loop using two 6mm jumprings, so that it faces forward.

Bracelet

YOU WILL NEED

1 x 22in (550mm) length of US 26-gauge (SWG 27, 0.4mm) antique brass wire

11 x 8mm Lucite beads

18 x 4mm glass or Lucite beads

2 x 3in (75mm) lengths of chunky chain

4 x 6mm jumprings

5 x 4mm jumprings

2 x 2in (50mm) antique brass headpins

1 x antique brass kilt pin with 3 loops

3 x antique brass or glass heart charms

Toggle clasp

Make a single bold heart and attach chain to either side with 6mm jumprings, then add to the theme with extra heart charms in metal or glass. Attach a toggle clasp at the ends of the chain with 6mm jumprings. Make up two beaded headpins, using any spare beads, then attach to the toggle loop. Add heart charms using the 4mm jumprings randomly around the bracelet.

Navaho Beads

Dream catch the world of Native America with these beaded projects by Irene McCarthy inspired by the colors and patterns of Native American knitwear.

FOR THE NECKLACE YOU WILL NEED

2 x toggle clasps, silver-colored

1 x 25mm beaded ring link, silver-colored

20in (500mm) fine soft-flex beading wire, silver

2 x 1.5mm x 2mm silver crimp tubes

79in (2m) US 28-gauge (SWG 30, 0.3mm) wire, silver

1 x 6mm turquoise pearl

1 x 6mm open jumprings

10g x 2.5mm (size 8) seed beads, red

10g x 2.5mm (size 8) seed beads, blue

10g x 2.5mm (size 8) seed beads, black

Flush cutters

Crimper

Flat-nose pliers

Chain-nose pliers

Ruler

Beading mat

Necklace

1   Place the large ring and three red and three blue seed beads onto the beading mat. Using 20in (500mm) of the US 28-gauge (SWG 30, 0.3mm) wire, attach one end securely to the ring. Neaten the end. Work the wire across the ring, threading a bead randomly onto the wire and weaving in and out to create a floating look. Secure, snip off any excess wire and use the nylon pliers to make sure there are no sharp edges.

2   For the main tassel, cut a strand of the US 28-gauge wire and secure to the ring as before. Thread four blue, five red, four blue, five red and a black seed bead onto the wire. Thread the wire back through the seed beads (missing the last black bead) to secure them. Pull until the wire end is near the ring. Secure and snip off any excess wire and use the flat-nose pliers to prevent sharp edges.

3   To make the next left and right tassels, work out from the center tassel. Thread four blue, five red, four blue, two red and a black seed bead onto the wire. For the next two tassels, use four blue, five red, four blue, two red and one black seed bead. For next adjoining tassels use four blue, five red, two blue and a black seed bead.

4   Cut 8in (200mm) of US 28-gauge wire and bend in half. Secure onto the top of the large ring. Thread a black and a red seed bead, a pearl, and a red and a black seed bead onto both strands of wire. Wire wrap one wire either side of the bottom section of the toggle until secure. Leave a small gap between the wires. With the ends of the wire, work crossing over downward, and around the beads until you reach the bottom. Secure and snip off any excess.

5   To create the seed bead necklace cut 20in (500mm) of soft-flex wire. Thread one end through the top loop on the toggle and crimp into place. Add seed beads in the pattern of the main tassel until the length you require is achieved. Thread through the crimp to secure it onto the bar part of the toggle. Hide the tail through a few seed beads.

6   Take one open jumpring and thread through the main loop on the wind charm loop and close it into place. Thread the necklace through the jumpring to complete the whole necklace design.

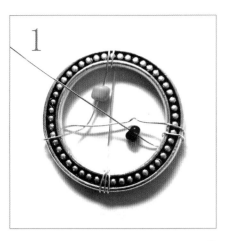

2

4

6

Earrings

YOU WILL NEED

2 x 20mm beaded ring links, silver-colored

197in (5m) US 28-gauge (SWG 30, 0.3mm) wire, silver

6 x 6mm open jumprings

2 x flat hook earwires

30 x 2.5mm (size 8) seed beads, red

42 x 2.5mm (size 8) seed beads, blue

10 x 2.5mm (size 8) seed beads, black

Create a matching set of earrings using the smaller-size ring link by following the same steps as for the main part of the necklace. To finish, simply open two 6mm jumprings and thread through the loop and close the rings. Thread on another 6mm jumpring and attach to the loop of the earring, close to secure. Make two.

Bracelet

YOU WILL NEED

1 x toggle clasp, silver-colored

1 x 25mm beaded ring link, silver-colored

4 x 3–1 beaded links

39⅜in (1m) US 26-gauge (SWG 27, 0.4mm) soft-flex wire, silver

12 x 1.5mm x 2mm crimp tubes, silver

39⅜in (1m) US 28-gauge (SWG 30, 0.3mm) wire, silver

4 x 6mm open jumprings

38 x 2.5mm (size 8) seed beads, red

38 x 2.5mm (size 8) seed beads, blue

38 x 2.5mm (size 8) seed beads, black

Make the central section of the bracelet using Step 1 and add jumprings either side. Use a 3–1 beaded link and crimp soft-flex wire to each of the three-loop sides. String three equal lengths of seed beads (size to fit your wrist) and attach the ends to another 3–1 beaded link. Repeat for the other side of the central ring and attach the connectors to the ring with the jumprings. Add a toggle clasp to finish.

Jumpring Spacer

Use up your leftover beads and buttons in Clair Wolfe's pretty spacer bracelets. They are based on a clever design by Lesley Watt, and the technique will add a new dimension to your beadwork projects.

FOR THE FLOWER BRACELET YOU WILL NEED

1 x 15mm button or large flower bead

1 x roll of beading thread

2 x beading needles

2 x 4mm crystals

35 x 10–12mm crystal beads (mixed selection works well)

30 x seed beads

35 x 6mm closed jumprings

Craft glue

Scissors

Flower bracelet

1 Cut a manageable length of beading thread and add a beading needle onto each of the ends (big-eye needles are perfect for this). Pass one needle through the flower and a small crystal, and then back through the flower, pull the thread and secure the flower with the crystal at the halfway point on the thread. Pass both needle and threads through the first bead.

2 Pass one of the needle and threads through a bead, then pass both of the needles and threads through a jumpring. Pass the second needle and thread through a bead, once again followed by both being passed through a jumpring. Keep adding beads and jumprings in the same manner until the bracelet has reached the desired length.

3 Most bracelets are between 7in (180mm) and 8in (200mm), depending on the size of the wearer's wrist and the desired drape of the bracelet. Place the bracelet around the wrist to see if it is the correct size. Add more beads and jumprings, or remove some beads and jumprings until satisfied with the overall length. Remember that the clasp will add about 1in (25mm) in length.

4 Use seed beads in a complementary color to create a clasp. Thread several on to each of the needles and threads, enough to create a loop big enough for the flower to fit through—try to make as tight a fit as possible for a secure clasp.

5 Next, thread both needles through two beads—one large, one small— then pass the needles back through the larger of the beads.

6 Thread one of the needles back through one of the strands of small seed beads, and the second needle through the remaining strand of seed beads. Remove the needles, then pull on the threads until they are neat and taught. Tie several knots to secure and finish with a dab of glue. Leave to dry before snipping away the excess thread.

This technique can be used to create longer lengths, which are perfect for necklaces.

Make sure all your jumprings are closed for a neater look.

Button bracelet

YOU WILL NEED

Button

1 x 30in (760mm) length of waxed cotton or linen cord

68 x 4–4.5mm (size 5) seed beads plus extra for the cord ends

68 x 5mm closed jumprings

Take a length of waxed cotton or linen cord and thread it through the holes of a button. Pull the cords so that the button is centered and both lengths are equal. Tie a knot as close to the button as possible, then start to thread a bead onto one of the cord lengths, followed by a jumpring onto both. Thread a second bead on the second cord, then a jumpring, and repeat until the desired length is reached. It takes about 68 seed beads to make a 7½in (190mm) bracelet, so adjust as needed. Tie a knot close to the last bead, plus a second one to create a loop to fit over the button. Thread extra beads onto the cord ends, knot to secure, and trim off any excess cord.

Jet Set

Travel light for your holiday this summer with a fabulous set of interchangeable bracelets and necklaces with matching accessories by Linda Brumwell.

FOR THE NECKLACE YOU WILL NEED

1 x 16in (405mm) strand 3mm rondelles, frosted amethyst

2 x 16in (405mm) strands 5mm small nuggets, turquoise

1 x 16in strand (405mm) 2mm coral nuggets, fuchsia

1 x 16in strand (405mm) 2mm coral nuggets, green

1 x 16in (405mm) strand 8mm abalone small nuggets

6 x 7mm closed jumprings, silver

5 x 10mm spiral brass balls, silver-colored

12 x 2mm crimp beads, silver

1 x roll of 0.38mm beading thread, stainless steel

3 x large bolt-ring clasps

3 x bolt-ring clasps, silver

Crimping pliers

Side cutters

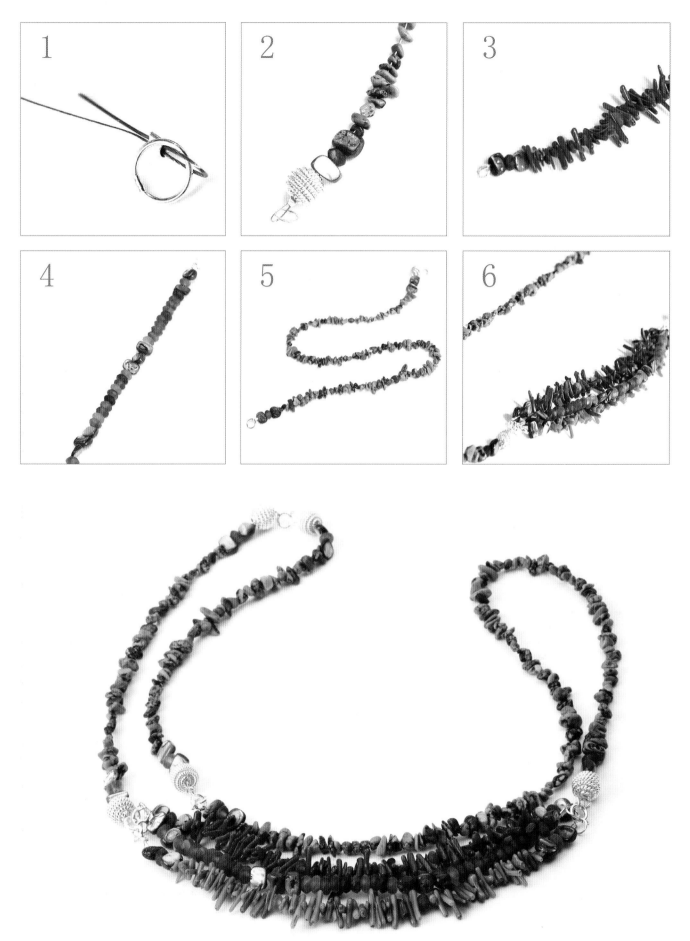

Necklace

1   Take 10in (250mm) of thread and add on a crimp and a 7mm jumpring. Return the thread through the crimp, close (see page 21), and trim off any excess. Thread a spiral bead, an abalone, an amethyst, and an abalone.

2   Thread turquoise nuggets for approx. 5½in (140mm) followed by an abalone, an amethyst, an abalone, and a spiral bead. Thread a crimp bead and a bolt-ring clasp. Secure as before, and trim any excess. Two of this style have been made here.

3   Using 10in (250mm) of thread, secure a small bolt-ring clasp using a crimp bead as before. Thread an abalone, an amethyst and an abalone. Then thread 25 purple coral, one amethyst, 25 coral, one amethyst, 25 coral, an abalone, an amethyst and a final abalone followed by a crimp, and a small jumpring. Secure as before and trim any excess. Make another using the green coral.

4   Using Step 3 for guidance, make another bracelet but instead of the coral use ten amethyst, three abalone, ten amethyst, three abalone, and ten amethyst (42 beads in total). Finish off the same way as the previous step.

5   Using 20in (510mm) of thread attach a large bolt-ring clasp using a crimp as before. Thread a spiral bead, an abalone, an amethyst, and an abalone. Continue to thread turquoise nuggets for around 15in (380mm) followed by an abalone, an amethyst, and another abalone. Attach a large jumpring with a crimp as before.

6   Join the two turquoise lengths together using the relevant clasps. Join the two coral and the amethyst and abalone lengths to the jumpring on one of the turquoise lengths using the three bolt-ring clasps. Attach the long length of turquoise to all three bolt rings on the previous three lengths. Join the final clasps together to form a long necklace. This can be used in many different ways for necklaces and bracelets depending on how they are attached and detached.

Earrings

YOU WILL NEED

6 x 3mm rondelles, frosted amethyst

2 x 5mm small nuggets, turquoise

2 x 8mm abalone small nuggets

6 x 7mm jumprings, silver

2 x 10mm spiral brass balls, silver-colored

2 x small bolt-ring clasps

2 x 1in (25mm) eyepins, silver

6 x 1in (25mm) headpins, silver

2 x earwires

Attach a turquoise nugget to an earwire using an eyepin. Attach a small bolt-ring clasp to the eyepin. Make several detachable "charms" using beads and headpins and place them on jumprings to make a medley of different matching earrings. Secure on the headpins with wrapped loops (see page 18).

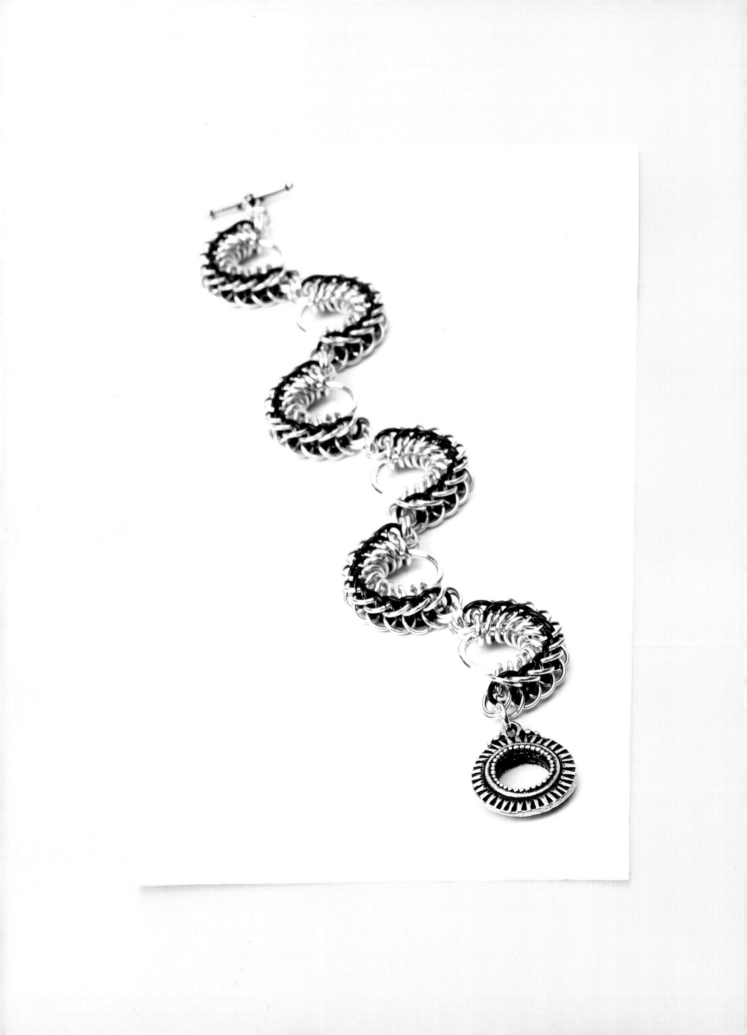

Round Maille Curves

Emphasize the curves of these chainmaille components by using contrasting jumprings to make this unusual and striking set by Sarah Austin.

FOR THE BRACELET YOU WILL NEED

144 x anodized aluminum jumprings, inner diameter 4.2mm, 0.81mm, silver (A)

82 x anodized aluminum jumprings, inner diameter 3.8mm, 1mm, silver (B)

60 x anodized aluminum jumprings, inner diameter 5.2mm, 1mm, black (C)

6 x anodized aluminum jumprings, inner diameter 10.2mm, 1.6mm, silver (D)

1 x sunburst toggle, 17 x 21mm, silver-plated

2 x chain-nose or flat-nose pliers

Bracelet

1 The red ring is the jumpring being added in each step. Close 24 of ring (A) and open eleven of ring (B) (see page 16). Link four (A) rings with one ring (B). You may find it helpful to also link an eyepin or paper clip. Lay out the rings as shown.

2 Link one (B) ring down through the two lower left-hand rings (A), and then up through the lower right-hand ring (A). Add two more rings (A) before closing ring (B). Lay out the rings as shown. Continue adding pairs of rings in this way until you have joined 24 rings (A).

3 Open ten (C) rings. Pinch the lower end of the chain between your thumb and forefinger so that the pairs of (A) rings form a "V"-shape. Link one ring (C) through the intersection of the first two pairs of (A) rings and then through the center of the third pair of (A) rings.

4 Link one (C) ring through the intersection of the next two pairs of (A) rings and then through the center of the following pair of (A) rings. The ring just added sits on top of the previous (C) ring. Continue joining with (C) rings in this way until you have linked ten (C) rings.

5 Link one (D) ring through eleven (B) rings, which are beneath the black (C) rings added in Step 4. This will stiffen the short round maille chain. Close the ring (D) and turn it so that you hide the join within the (B) rings. Repeat Steps 1–5 to make six round maille components.

6 Using two (B) rings, join two components by linking one pair of (A) rings at the end of each curve. Make sure you alternate the direction of the curves. Attach the toggle ring with one (B) ring. At the other end of the bracelet, link a chain of two pairs of (B) rings. Attach the toggle bar to the last pair of rings with one (B) ring.

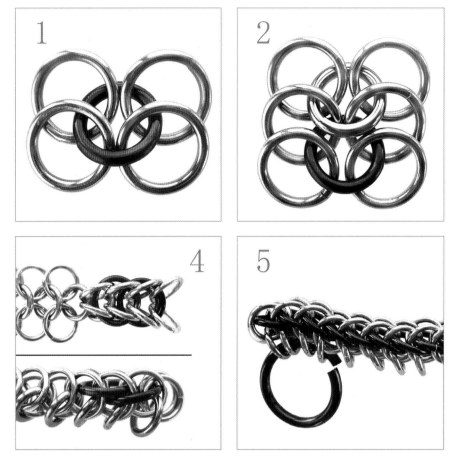

After adding each pair of rings in Step 2, pat the maille with your finger to reposition the links. If your work does not lie well, it is probably because a ring is incorrectly linked.

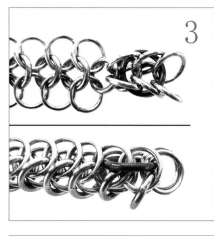

Earrings

YOU WILL NEED

48 x anodized aluminum jumprings, inner diameter 4.2mm, 0.81mm, silver (A)

28 x anodized aluminum jumprings, inner diameter 3.8mm, 1mm, silver (B)

20 x anodized aluminum jumprings, inner diameter 5.2mm, 1mm, black (C)

2 x anodized aluminum jumprings, inner diameter 10.2mm, 1.6mm, silver (D)

4 x 1in (25mm) eyepins, silver-plated

2 x earwires, silver-plated

Make two maille components. Link an eyepin to the pairs of rings (B) at each end of the curve. Make a second loop about ⅝in (15mm) from the eyepin loop. Link the two loops together with one ring (B) and attach to an earwire.

Pendant

YOU WILL NEED

24 x anodized aluminum jumprings, inner diameter 4.2mm, 0.81mm, silver (A)

13 x anodized aluminum jumprings, inner diameter 3.8mm, 1mm, silver (B)

10 x anodized aluminum jumprings, inner diameter 5.2mm, 1mm, black (C)

1 x anodized aluminum jumprings, inner diameter 10.2mm, 1.6mm, silver (D)

3 x 2in (50mm) headpins silver-plated

10 x 4mm jet bicone crystals

4 x 6mm jet bicone crystals

9 x 5mm faceted spacers

1 x black cord necklace

Make beaded dangles using 4mm and 6mm jet bicone crystals and three 5mm faceted spacers. Make two headpins with one spacer, one 6mm bicone, one spacer, two 4mm bicones, one spacer, and one 4mm bicone. Make one headpin with one 6mm bicone, one spacer, two 4mm bicones, one spacer, one 6mm bicone, one spacer, and two 4mm bicones. Make a maille component and attach the dangles to the last three jumprings on one end. Attach the other end to the necklace using two jumprings.

Feeling Hot

Make this vibrant jewelry set by Gemma Reilly with a few simple techniques. Add it to your holiday wardrobe and you will be as hot as the sunshine!

FOR THE NECKLACE YOU WILL NEED

20 x flat cord ends, gold-plated

1 x 118in (3m) length of ⅛in (2.5mm) suede, rich red

24 x 5mm jumprings, gold-plated

1 x 39⅜in (1m) length of light chain, gold-plated

1 x 39⅜in (1m) length of trace chain, gold-plated

7 x 1in (25mm) gold-plated eyepins

1 x trigger clasp, gold-plated

7 x 15mm matt wood beads, crimson

Round-nose pliers

Chain-nose pliers

Side cutters

Scissors

Necklace

1 Cut 20 lengths of suede, each 4in (100mm) long. Fold each side of a cord end in slightly and place the end of one of the lengths of suede inside it, then with the flat part of the multi pliers squeeze it flat (see page 18). Repeat for 19 more. Trim the ends at an angle with a sharp pair of scissors.

2 Cut a length of light chain with 20 links. Open a 5mm jumpring (see page 16) and join one length of suede to the end link. Repeat along the length of chain. Make sure your crimps all face the same way for a neat finish.

3 Open the loop on an eyepin, attach to the end link of the fringed chain and close the loop. Thread on a wooden bead, trim ⅜in (10mm) above the bead. Bend into a loop (see page 20), attach the loop of the next eyepin, and then close the loop. Continue in this way until you have added six wooden beads to one side of the fringing.

4 Attach a 2¾in (70mm) length of chain to the last beaded eyepin, and add a jumpring with a trigger clasp to the end of the chain.

5 Cut two 7½in (190mm) lengths of light chain and one 7½in (190mm) length of trace chain. Join the three ends together with a 5mm jumpring and add another jumpring.

6 Twist the chains loosely around each other. Open the loop of an eyepin and attach the ends of the chain, then close the loop. Thread on a wooden bead, trim ⅜in (10mm) above the bead, bend into a loop, and attach to the end loop of the fringed chain. Close the loop.

Make sure you close your jumprings tightly for a professional finish.

Try making the set in black and white with black antique findings to add a statement to your favorite outfit. For an even bolder look, add extra wire-wrapped beads.

Bracelet

YOU WILL NEED

4 x 5mm jumprings, gold-plated

10 x 1in (25mm) eyepins, gold-plated

1 x trigger clasp, gold-plated

10 x 15mm matt wood beads, crimson

Make a chain of ten beaded eyepins in the same way as the necklace. Attach a jumpring with a trigger clasp to one end and a chain of three jumprings to the other.

Earrings

YOU WILL NEED

10 x flat cord end, gold-plated

1 x 39⅜in (1m) length of ⅛in (2.5mm) suede, rich red

10 x 5mm jumprings, gold-plated

2 x 1in (25mm) eyepins, gold-plated

1 x 2in (50mm) length of light chain, gold-plated

2 x trigger clasps, gold-plated

2 x long ballwires, gold-plated

19 x 15mm matt wood beads, crimson

Cut a length of light chain with five links and attach cord ends to five lengths of suede. Join each length to a link in the chain with a jumpring. Trim the ends at an angle. Open the loop of an eyepin, attach it to the end link of chain, and thread on a bead. Trim ⅜in (10mm) above the bead, bend into a loop, attach the long ballwire, and close the loop. Repeat to make a pair.

Rainbow Bright

No clasps are needed when you use stretchy o-rings in these colorful chainmaille weaves by Sarah Austin. Incorporating metal rings in the same color as the o-rings gives each of the individual designs great impact.

FOR THE DOUBLE BRACELET YOU WILL NEED

72 x EPDM o-rings, internal diameter 6.4mm, 1.63mm in rainbow colors—12 each of red, orange, yellow, green, blue, and purple

144 x anodized aluminum, saw-cut jumprings, internal diameter 6.8mm, 1.6mm in rainbow colors—24 each of red, orange, yellow, green, blue, and purple (A)

18 x anodized aluminum saw-cut jumprings, internal diameter 10.2mm, 1.6mm in rainbow colors—3 each of red, orange, yellow, green, blue, and purple (B)

2 x pairs of chain-nose, flat-nose, or bent-nose pliers

Bangle

1 Link three pairs of each rainbow color o-ring into a 2–1–2 chain using one ring (A) of the same color. Join the next o-ring color using a ring (A) that matches the first of the two o-ring colors. The color order is: red, orange, yellow, green, blue, and purple.

2 Open six rings (A) of each color (see page 16). Lay out your chain and push the first top o-ring downward—this will be referred to as the top o-ring. Link two rings (A) down through the upper half of the bottom o-ring, taking it underneath the two o-rings, and weaving it up through the lower half of the top o-ring. Repeat with each pair of o-rings using matching colored rings (A).

3 Open three rings (A) of each color. Separate the first pair of rings (A) added in Step 2. Link one ring (A) between these two rings, making sure the ring (A) weaves through the intersection of the two o-rings at the center. Using matching colored rings (A), continue adding one ring to each unit.

4 Repeat Steps 1–3, except for Step 2, where you will need to push the top o-ring upwards before adding the pair of rings (A). This is so that the second chain is a mirror image of the first chain. Lay out the two chains with the lower o-rings facing toward the center.

5 Open three rings (B) of each color. Link one ring (B) between each pair of rings (A) added in Step 2, making sure the ring (B) weaves through the intersection of the two o-rings at the center. You may find it easier to weave the ring (B) using your fingers before closing with pliers. Continue joining the two chains using matching rings (B).

6 Open two purple rings (A). To join the doubled chain into a bangle, weave one purple ring (A) through the central intersection of the end purple o-rings and end red o-rings. Repeat to join the second part of the doubled chain.

To make the bangle smaller, reduce blocks of color evenly. For example, have two blue and orange (on opposite sides) or two purple, green, and orange (alternate).

Pendant

YOU WILL NEED

14 x EPDM o-rings, internal diameter 6.4mm, 1.63mm in rainbow colors—2 each of red, orange, green, blue, purple and 4 of yellow

35 x anodized aluminum, saw-cut jumprings, internal diameter 6.8mm, 1.6mm in rainbow colors—5 each of red, orange, green, blue, purple and 10 of yellow (A)

1 x anodized aluminum saw-cut jumprings, internal diameter 10.2mm, 1.6mm in red (B)

1 x finished cord necklace

Follow Steps 1–3, making two yellow units and one unit of each of the other colors. Repeat Step 3 on the opposite side of four of the units using matching rings (A). Link one ring (B) through the four rings (A) just added. Repeat Step 3 for the remaining three units, linking them to the ring (B). Join the seven units into a circle as in Step 6. Open the outer purple ring and attach to the necklace, close the jumpring to finish.

Single bangle

YOU WILL NEED

36 x EPDM o-rings, internal diameter 6.4mm, 1.63mm in rainbow colors—6 each of red, orange, yellow, green, blue, and purple

90 x anodized aluminum, saw-cut jumprings, internal diameter 6.8mm, 1.6mm in rainbow colors—15 each of red, orange, yellow, green, blue, and purple (A)

Follow Steps 1–3 to the required length. Repeat Step 3 linking matching colored rings (A) on the opposite side of the pairs of rings (A) added in Step 2.

Beautiful in Blue

Blue pearls in different shades are the inspiration behind these designs by Gemma Reilly—a perfect set to wear for the summer season.

FOR THE NECKLACE YOU WILL NEED

2 x 3½oz (100g) glass pearl mix, blue tones (bead sizes 4mm to 12mm)

15 x 16mm glass pearls, dark blue

12 x crimps, silver-plated

12 x crimp covers, silver-plated

1 x roll of 32ft (10m) flexible plastic-coated wire, silver-colored

4 x 8mm jumprings, silver-plated

1 x trigger clasp, silver-plated

1 x 3ft (1m) length of heavy chain, silver-plated

Round-nose pliers

Chain-nose pliers

Crimping pliers

Side cutters

Necklace

1. Cut 7in (180mm) of plastic-coated wire. Thread the end through a crimp, bend it into a loop, and pass it back through the crimp. Squeeze with the hole nearest the plier handles to make a "V" shape. Use the other hole on the pliers to make it round. Add a crimp cover (see page 21).

2. Open your bags of pearls and separate them into the different shades. Thread a 4in (100mm) row of light blue beads, starting small, getting bigger, then back to small beads onto the wire.

3. Thread a crimp onto the wire after the beads, pass the end of the wire back through the crimp, and pull tight to create a loop. Squeeze the crimp in the same way. Trim the excess wire and add a crimp cover. You need one more in the light blue, two rows in the dark shade, and one row in a medium shade.

4. Cut 15¾in (400mm) of wire. Add a crimp and crimp cover to one end. Thread on a dark blue bead around 12mm, a 16mm bead, and the loop of a dark blue section. Add two more 16mm beads, a pale blue section, and another two 16mm beads. Next pass through the second loop of the dark blue section.

5. Add a 16mm bead, the medium shade blue section, and a 16mm bead, then pass through the second loop of the pale blue section. Add the center bead. Continue to mirror the first half of the necklace. Add a crimp to the wire, pass the end of the wire back through the crimp, and pull tight to create a loop. Squeeze the crimp. Trim the excess wire and add a crimp cover.

6. Cut two 7in (180mm) lengths of chain. Attach each length to the beaded section with an 8mm jumpring. Add an 8mm jumpring to one remaining end and an 8mm jumpring with a trigger clasp to the other.

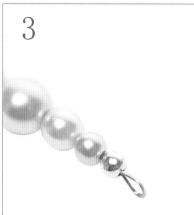

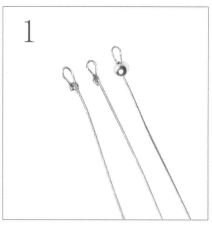

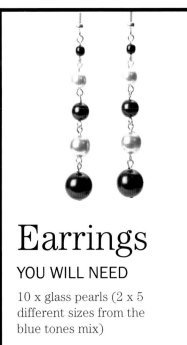

Earrings

YOU WILL NEED

10 x glass pearls (2 x 5 different sizes from the blue tones mix)

2 x headpins, silver-plated

8 x eyepins, silver-plated

2 x long ballwires, silver-plated

Choose five beads in ascending size for one earring and repeat for the other earring. Thread the largest onto a headpin. Trim ⅜in (10mm) above the bead, bend into a loop, add an eyepin, and close the loop. Add the next size down bead, trim the eye pin ⅜in in (10mm) above the bead, bend into a loop, add another eyepin and squeeze closed. Continue to make a chain of beads, reducing in size. Add a long ballwire to the last loop. Repeat to make the pair.

Bracelet

YOU WILL NEED

1 x 3½oz (100g) glass pearl mix, blue tones

100 x headpins, silver-plated

2 x 8mm jumprings, silver-plated

1 x trigger clasp, silver-plated

1 x 7in (180mm) length of heavy chain, silver-plated

Cut 7in (180mm) of chain. Add an 8mm jumpring to one end and an 8mm jumpring with a trigger clasp to the other. Thread a bead onto a headpin, trim ⅜in (10mm) above the bead, bend into a loop, and attach to the chain. Close the loop. Repeat to add as many beads as you like to the bracelet.

Out of Africa

Make this bold, African-inspired jewelry by Gemma Reilly using simple plaiting techniques, and customize it with beads of your choice.

FOR THE NECKLACE YOU WILL NEED

34 x 4mm x 5mm barrel beads, gold-plated

23 x 5mm x 6mm barrel beads, gold-plated

1 x 118in (3m) length of thick leather, brown

23 x 5mm lustred round beads, emerald

6 x cord ends, gold-plated

1 x 12in (300mm) length of heavy chain, gold-plated

26 x 8mm jumprings, gold-plated

2 x 5mm jumprings, gold-plated

23 x headpins, gold-plated

1 x trigger clasp, gold-plated

Round-nose pliers

Chain-nose pliers

Side cutters

Scissors

When plaiting, take your time to make sure the plait is flat but also curves nicely to form the necklace shape.

This style of plaiting leather cord with beads would work with any size of bead, as long as they have a hole large enough for the cord to fit through.

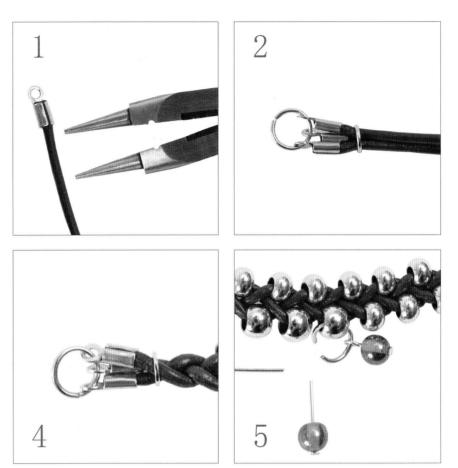

Necklace

1 Cut three 20in (500mm) lengths of leather. Place the end of one of the lengths into the cord end—squeeze each side in slightly. Squeeze it flat with the flat part of the multi pliers (see page 18). Repeat for the two other pieces.

2 Open an 8mm jumpring, attach the three pieces of leather and close. Thread the three lengths through the middle of a 5mm jumpring—this can be a bit of a squeeze. Move the jumpring along the leather so that it sits nicely underneath the cord ends.

3 Attach the 8mm jumpring to something sturdy, such as your trouser leg. Plait the leather tightly. When you have ⅜in (10mm) plaited, add a 4mm bead to the right-hand strand. Continue to plait, and add a 4mm bead to the left-hand strand. Continue this way until you have added three 4mm beads to the right-hand side. Now add the larger beads—you need 23 large beads and three more small beads on the right hand side, and 28 small beads on the left. This will make the curve.

4 Plait ⅜in (10mm) of the leather after the beads. Trim the leather with a sharp pair of scissors ⅛in (2mm) longer than the finished plait. Thread on a 5mm jumpring and add the cord ends in the same way. Join the three ends with an 8mm jumpring.

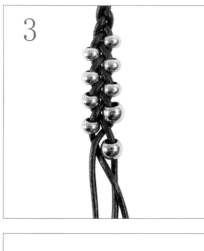

3

6

Earrings

2 x 4mm x 5mm barrel beads, gold-plated

2 x 5mm x 6mm barrel beads, gold-plated

2 x 5mm lustred round beads, emerald

6 x 8mm jumprings, gold-plated

2 x headpins, gold-plated

2 x earwires, gold-plated

Open an 8mm jumpring, add an earwire, and a 4mm spacer. Close the jumpring. Thread another jumpring through the 4mm spacer and add a 5mm spacer. Close the jumpring. Add a final jumpring to the bottom and a beaded headpin. Close the jumpring. Repeat to make a pair.

5 Thread a bead onto a headpin and trim ⅜in (10mm) above the bead. Use the tip of the pliers to bend the headpin into a loop and close. Open an 8mm jumpring, add the beaded headpin. Thread the jumpring through the first of the large beads on your plaited section. Add a beaded headpin to every large bead in the same way.

6 Cut two 6in (150mm) lengths of chain and attach one to each end of the plaited section using the 8mm jumprings. Add an 8mm jumpring to the remaining ends of the chain and add a trigger clasp to one side.

Bracelet

20 x 4mm x 5mm barrel beads, gold-plated

16 x 5mm x 6mm barrel beads, gold-plated

1 x 39⅜in (1m) length of thick leather, brown

1 x 5mm lustred round beads, emerald

6 x cord ends, gold-plated

5 x 8mm jumprings, gold-plated

2 x 5mm jumprings, gold-plated

1 x headpin, gold-plated

1 x trigger clasp, gold-plated

Make the bracelet in the same way as the necklace, using three 11¾in (300mm) lengths but start with a 4mm bead on the right, and a 4mm bead on the left, then a 5mm bead on the right and left. Continue plaiting like this until you have added 18 x 4mm beads and 16 x 5mm beads. Add the 5mm jumpring and cord ends in the same way. Add an 8mm jumpring and a trigger clasp to one side and a chain of four 8mm jumprings to the other. Add a beaded headpin to the last jumpring.

Ocean Depths

Take the colors of the deep ocean and weave them together to create these stunning complementary designs by Sian Hamilton.

FOR THE NECKLACE YOU WILL NEED

1 x roll of heavy beading cord

1,800 (or around 100g) x 3.3mm (size 6) seed beads: cobalt frosted, sky-lined white, and blue iris

1 x clasp (use metal color of your choice)

18 x crimp beads

18 x 3mm jumprings

2 x 5mm jumprings

2 x 6mm jumprings

2 x 15mm wide x 18mm high filigree bead caps, cone-shaped

2 x 2in (50mm) eyepins

Crimping or any flat-jaw pliers

Chain-nose pliers

Necklace

1 Cut a 23⅝in (600mm) length of beading cord. Take a crimp bead, thread on, and add a 3mm jumpring. Bring the cord back through the crimp bead and close. You could use crimping pliers to make a neat finish, but any flat-jaw pliers will work as well.

2 Thread on 200 seed beads. Size 6 gives a chunky look, but this necklace style works with any size of bead. You'll need more beads if using smaller ones or fewer if going larger.

3 When you have strung all the beads, take another crimp bead and jumpring to finish the open end, as you did in Step 1. Make nine strands, exactly the same length. Three colors have been used for this necklace, but you can use any color combination that suits you.

4 Take a 6mm jumpring, open it and attach all nine strands. Feed on the strands, keeping the same colors together. Add an eyepin and close the jumpring.

5 Using masking tape, tape the eyepin with the strands attached to your work surface. This should hold it in place. Taking the three color strands (with like colors together), plait the necklace, keeping the plaiting slightly loose. If it's too tight the necklace won't sit nicely on the neck. When you get to the end, hold the plait and attach to the other 6mm jumpring along with another eyepin.

6 Add a bead cap to each eyepin to hide the ends, then using chain-nose pliers, grab the wire coming out of the cap and turn a right-angle bend about ⅛in (2mm) above the cap. Make a wrapped loop (see page 18)—the space below the right angle is where you will wrap the wire to complete the loop. Add a clasp to one end with a 5mm jumpring and the other 5mm jumpring to the other to complete the necklace.

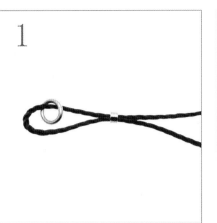

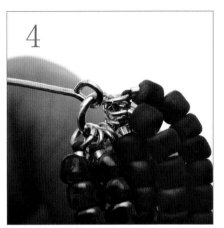

This design is versatile and easy to play around with. As all the findings are kept open until you wrap the loop at the cone end, you can experiment with colors and strands to get a look that suits you.

Earrings

YOU WILL NEED

1 x roll of heavy beading cord

400 x size 6 seed beads, cobalt frosted, sky-lined white, and blue iris

18 x size 8 seed beads in a complementary color

18 x crimp beads

18 x 3mm jumprings

2 x 6mm jumprings

2 x 15mm wide x 18mm high filigree bead caps, cone-shaped

2 x 2in (50mm) eyepins

2 x earwires

Create earrings by making nine different length strands of beads and hanging them from filigree bead caps. To make the strands, take a length of beading cord and use Steps 1 and 2 of the main project to make nine different length strands. On the end of each strand, make a loop, add a crimp bead, close the crimp with pliers, and cut off the beading cord as close to the crimp as possible. Add all nine strands to a 6mm jumpring, with an eyepin. Follow Step 6 to add a bead cap, then add an earwire to the wrapped loop at the top of the cap. Repeat these instructions to make a second earring.

Fine necklace

YOU WILL NEED

1 x roll of light beading cord

1 x beading needle

100g x size 11 seed beads in three complementary colors

1 x clasp and jumpring (use metal color of your choice)

18 x crimp beads

2 x 5mm jumprings

2 x large calottes

1 x 10in (250mm) of medium-weight open-link chain

Beading needle

Make a finer version of this necklace using size 11 seed beads. You will need to use a beading needle to thread the beads onto the strands. Take a length of beading cord and thread on a crimp bead. Close the crimp about 3in (75mm) from the end of the thread. Thread on beads to make a 12in (305mm) strand then thread on another crimp and close it. Cut the thread about 3in (75mm) beyond the crimp bead. Repeat this to make nine strands of the same length, using three different colors of bead. When all the strands are finished, gather them together and thread all nine strands through the hole in a large calotte. Knot all the strands together inside the calotte cup and close the calotte with pliers. Now tape down that calotte cup as in Step 5 and plait the strands together. Gather all the strands together at the other end when the plait is done and thread them through the other calotte. Knot and close the cup as before. Add the 5mm jumprings to the two calottes and add on the 10in (250mm) chain. Find the center of the chain and open the jumpring at that point. Add a clasp to the open ring and close. The last link on the other end of the chain will be used as the closer for the clasp.

Vibrant Fuchsia

Make this stunning floral jewelry set by Debbie Kershaw using stringing and simple bead-sewing techniques. Create a riot of color with Lucite flower beads for a truly fun design.

FOR THE BRACELET YOU WILL NEED

1 x roll of 7-strand beading wire, gold

1 x roll of nylon bead thread, white

1 x butterfly charm, antique gold

1 x extender chain, antique gold

1 x jumpring, antique gold

1 x headpin, antique gold

2 x crimp beads, antique gold

1 x trigger clasp, antique gold

Lampwork beads, green and orange

Selection of colored seed beads

3 x Lucite flowers

Selection of glass and wooden beads: fuchsia, orange, and green

Beading needle

Chain-nose pliers

Four rows of fringes have been used, but for a fuller bracelet you can add as many as you like.

Earrings

YOU WILL NEED

2 x butterfly charms, antique gold

4 x eyepins, antique gold

4 x glass or wooden beads, fuchsia, orange, and green

2 x earwires, antique gold

Thread beads onto eyepins and make simple loops at the open ends (see page 20). Attach together and add butterfly charms at the bottom and earwires at the top.

Bracelet

1 Cut a generous bracelet length of beading wire with extra for crimping. Thread on a crimp bead and the clasp. Bring the beading wire back through the crimp and crimp in place (see page 21). String on the lampwork, wooden, and glass beads to your desired length—measure by trying it around your wrist. Add a crimp at the open end, leaving around 1in (25mm) between the last bead and the crimp. This will leave space along your string to comfortably add the fringes. Close the crimp.

2 Thread a beading needle with cotton beading thread. Thread your needle through the first bead on the strand and pull through, leaving a cotton tail long enough to knot into place later.

3 Thread five orange seed beads and one green onto your needle and push down the thread to meet the bracelet. Run your needle back down the orange beads leaving out the last one (the green one), which will be your stopper bead. Pull tightly and secure by threading your needle through the next bead on the bracelet. This makes the first fringe.

4 Continue adding fringes as in Step 3 up one side of the bracelet, varying the bead combinations used. When you reach the end, leave a cord tail to knot later. Thread your needle again and repeat the process down the other side of the bracelet. Finish by securely knotting the two threads at each end together and trim.

5 You now have two rows of fringes, and you are going to add another two using the bigger orange beads and the flowers. Repeat steps 1–4 but using one larger bead or flower and one seed bead acting as your stopper bead. Sew them into your design as before and knot and trim the threads in place when you have finished.

6 Add jumprings to the crimped ends with a lobster clasp at one end and an extender chain at the other for fastening. If you wish, you could also add a butterfly and a small beaded headpin dangle to the end of the chain, secured with a strong jumpring. Put a dab of glue on your knots for extra security.

1

2

3

4

5

6

If your thread gets tangled, don't be afraid to add a new one by trimming the existing one and knotting with the new thread.

Necklace

YOU WILL NEED

1 x roll of necklace-size memory wire

1 x butterfly charm, antique gold

1 x extender chain, antique gold

1 x jumpring, antique gold

1 x headpin, antique gold

1 x eyepin, antique gold

1 x trigger clasp, antique gold

Lampwork beads, green and orange

Selection of colored seed beads

Selection of glass and wooden beads, fuchsia, orange, and green

Memory-wire cutters

Make a matching necklace by threading leftover beads onto necklace memory wire (always cut memory wire with specialist memory-wire cutters). Make a beaded eyepin with bead cap on either side of a large bead. Make a simple loop at the open end (see page 20). Add a butterfly charm to one end of the eyepin and attach the other end to the center of the necklace. Make simple loops at both ends of the necklace memory wire. With jumprings, add a clasp to one end and a jumpring to the other (see page 16).

Picture
Perfect

Show off your favorite photos and an array of beads in these gorgeous designs by Lisa Floyd. Make them as pretty as a picture by experimenting with different beads and finishes.

FOR THE BROOCH YOU WILL NEED

1 x 2in (50mm) kilt pin with loops

1 x 1in (25mm) photo frame with acetate insert

1 x 14in (350mm) trace or curb chain

Selection of 2mm and 3mm plain round metal beads

2mm crimp beads

2in (50mm) soft headpins

1 x roll of US 26-gauge (SWG 27, 0.4mm) beading wire

Assortment of metal bead caps

1 x metal flower bead charm

Selection of assorted metal beads in various sizes (fluted, filigree, plain)

Selection of assorted metal beads, including flower and leaf shapes

1 x roll of US 24-gauge (SWG 25, 0.5mm) 7-strand bright tigertail thread

1 x 2-sided image, 1³⁄₁₆ x 1³⁄₁₆in (20 x 20mm)

Flat-nose pliers

Crimping or chain-nose pliers

Scissors

Brooch

1 Select glass beads in a range of shapes, sizes, and color tones, plus several metal beads in various shapes and finishes. Pick four main glass beads and loosely arrange them along with the kilt pin, frame, and chain to identify the lengths required. Aim for an overall length of chains and beads, left to right, of around 3½in (90mm), 2½in (60mm), 4in (100mm), and 3¼in (80mm) to give an asymmetric effect. Avoid symmetry when choosing and placing all the beads.

2 Turn the four main beads into droppers by combining with bead caps and 2mm metal beads on 50mm soft headpins and forming wrapped loops on each (see page 18). For the top-drilled beads, get creative by turning a headpin, a 2mm bead, and a decorative bead cap into a flower—using the rest of the headpin to make the wrapped loop. Open up the last link on the chain lengths and attach a relevant bead.

3 Use flat pliers to open up links. Attach each chain length directly onto the kilt pin in between the pin's loops, and the frame to the center loop with three chain links. Place a crimp bead onto the tigertail and thread through one kilt-pin loop, double back through the crimp. Pull down to give two good lengths ready to attach some beads, pushing the crimp up tightly. Secure with a crimping tool or chain-nose pliers (see page 21).

4 The remainder of the beads will sit along the tigertail. Choose smaller glass beads for the top area of the brooch, increasing in size toward the bottom, keeping spaces in between. Use metal beads on either side, securing a crimp bead under each to keep them in place. Gauge the lengths required in relation to the chain, keeping one length longer than the other on each section, and beads all positioned slightly differently.

5 Repeat this theme for each loop. Alter the lengths for the outer sections so they become gradually shorter, keeping the main feature beads the longest. Snip the tigertail under the last crimps on each section. Laying the pieces down flat will help judge where to place the beads and cut the thread. Create detail by adding a metal flower charm to the frame and intersperse the glass beads with various fancy metal beads.

6 Take five soft headpins and thread on a selection of glass beads, metal beads, and bead caps to create flower-style features. Choose smaller beads and flower shapes combined with metal bead caps to make each individual piece. Place 2mm metal beads at the back. The finished features should be similar in size when finished and need to fit comfortably on the kilt pin, threaded through each loop.

7 Decide where each feature will sit and starting with the end one, thread through a loop so the detail is at the front of the kilt pin. Hold in place and wrap the headpin tightly and neatly around the pin's bar at least twice before wrapping the remainder around the 2mm metal beads at the back of the feature. Use chain-nose pliers to pull tight. Repeat for each feature.

8 Use a generous length of US 26-gauge wire, starting at one end and leaving spare wire to finish later. Wrap very tightly around the kilt-pin bar, working in one direction and over-lapping the chain links as you reach them. Ensure the chain lengths sit properly on the pin and fall freely. Continue wrapping along the pin and neatly around each bead feature to keep them in place. Cut and wrap the wire neatly to finish.

9 The picture selection can include photos, original images, or free downloads from the Internet—the choice is yours. The brooch insert is around 1³⁄₁₆ x 1³⁄₁₆in (20 x 20mm). Some printers can do sample sizes that are ideal—you can copy and paste into a frame using a suitable computer program or get them printed at a photo shop. Select your images and use the plastic inserts as templates to cut to size.

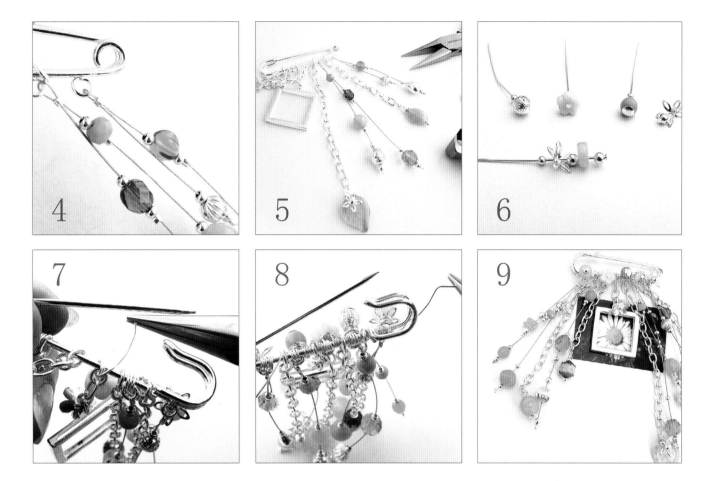

Bracelet

YOU WILL NEED

3 x 1in (25mm) 2-loop photo frames with acetate inserts

8 x oval jumprings

1 x toggle flower clasp

3 x dyed shell leaf beads

3 x 2in (50mm) eyepins

8 x 2in (50mm) headpins

8 x assorted glass and metal bead droppers and charms

This bracelet features photo frame links, leaves, bead, and metal charms and a stunning flower toggle clasp, all connected with oval links. Thread the leaf beads on to eyepins and create a simple loop at the ends of each pin (see page 20). Link two oval jumprings together (see page 16) and add one end of the clasp to one link, add a leaf bead to the other. With another oval jumpring, link the other end of the leaf bead to a photo frame. Continue to link the leaf beads and photo frames together using jumprings. Add the other pieces of the toggle clasp to the last photo frame using a jumpring. Make up eight beaded pieces using the headpins and create simple loops at the end. Add this to the oval jumprings, spreading them around the bracelet. Pick your favorite images to go in the frames, cut them to size, and place in the frames to complete the bracelet.

Brilliant Bows

Using crystals and pearls, make these dazzling designs created by Holly Fawcett, which are perfect for the party season. Muted and subtle tones give these pieces a vintage feel.

FOR THE NECKLACE YOU WILL NEED

18 x 6mm bicone crystals, antique pink

20 x 6mm pearls, powder almond

6 x 4mm bicone beads, antique pink

3 x 8mm faceted round beads, antique pink

2 x 5mm closed rings, black-plated

4 x 5mm jumprings, black-plated

2 x 1.5mm crimp beads, silver-plated

1 x 20in (500mm) length of medium curb chain, black-plated

1 x heart trigger clasp, black-plated

1 x 20in (500mm) length of US 26-gauge (SWG 27, 0.4mm) craft wire, non-tarnish silver-plated

Side cutters

Crimping or chain-nose pliers

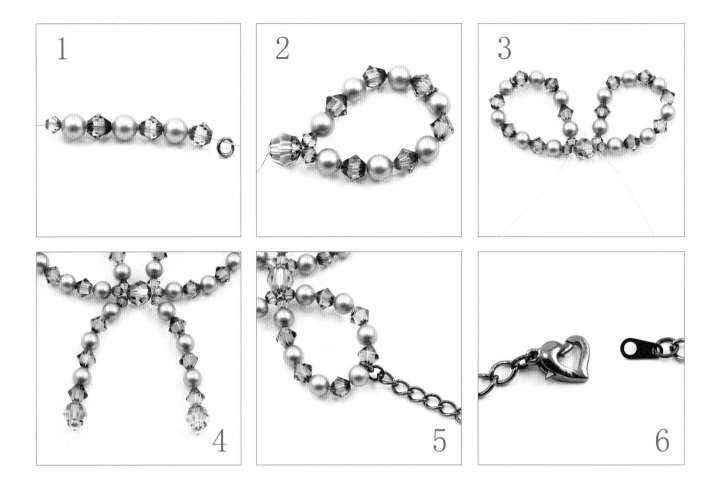

Necklace

1 Start by taking a piece of craft wire. Thread on a 4mm bicone bead, a 6mm pearl, a 6mm bicone crystal, a 6mm pearl, a 6mm bicone crystal, a 6mm pearl and then a 5mm closed ring.

2 Next, alternately thread on four more 6mm pearls and three more 6mm bicones, then another 4mm bicone to finish the first loop. Bring the two ends of wire together and thread them both through an 8mm faceted round crystal and pull tightly.

3 Using the longest piece of wire that comes out of the 8mm faceted bead, create a loop on the other side by repeating Steps 1 and 2. Thread the wire back though the 8mm faceted bead so that you have one length of wire protruding either side of the center bead.

4 Create the tails of the bow by threading on a 4mm bicone, three pearls and three 6mm bicones alternately, then a faceted round bead. Crimp this in place (see page 21) to secure and repeat on the other tail. Trim off any excess wire.

5 Use jumprings to attach your chain to the closed jumprings you threaded on while making the loops.

6 Finally, decide on how long you would like your necklace to be and cut to length. Add the clasp at the back with jumprings.

Once the bow is secured, you may have to mold it to shape so that both loops look the same and the bow sits flat to the neck.

For an alternative look, try using different colored chain and findings.

Earrings

YOU WILL NEED

32 x 4mm bicone crystals, antique pink

26 x 4mm pearls, powder almond

2 x 1.5mm crimp beads, silver-plated

1 x 20in (500mm) length of US 28-gauge (SWG 30, 0.3mm) craft wire, non-tarnish silver-plated

2 x flat pad post and back

E6000 glue

Make two matching bows, using 4mm beads and US 28-gauge (SWG 30, 0.3mm) wire. Then stick a flat stud to the back of the center bead.

Bracelet

YOU WILL NEED

60 x 4mm bicone crystals, antique pink

55 x 4mm pearls, powder almond

4 x 6mm pearls, powder almond

4 x 8mm faceted round beads, antique pink

16 x 4mm bead caps

9 x 5mm jumprings, black-plated

4 x 2in (50mm) headpins, black-plated

10 x 1.5mm crimp beads, silver-plated

1 x charm bracelet with toggle clasp, black-plated

1 x 20in (500mm) length of US 28 gauge (SWG 30, 0.3mm) craft wire, non-tarnish silver-plated

Round-nose pliers

Make five bows in the same way as in the main steps, only using smaller beads. Attach these evenly along a charm bracelet with jumprings (see page 16). Add extra decoration by using beads in the same colors and attach these using headpins; thread each headpin with a bead cap, 8mm round bead, bead cap, another bead cap, 6mm pearl and a final bead cap. Create simple loops at the ends of the headpins (see page 20) with round-nose pliers. Attach these beaded pieces in between the bows on the bracelet.

Bold Beads

Appealing in their simplicity, these beautiful beaded pieces by Gemma Reilly are quick and easy to make. Use these traditional techniques to create a contemporary addition to your jewelry box.

FOR THE NECKLACE YOU WILL NEED

27 x 5mm opaque lamp beads, white

16 x large (28 x 21mm) acrylic oval beads, blue and white

10 x 18mm acrylic round beads, blue and white

1 x 79in (2m) silk cord, thick, white (blue shown for clarity)

2 x calottes, silver-plated

2 x 8mm jumprings, silver-plated, side closing

1 x 15mm trigger clasp, silver-plated

Round-nose pliers

Chain-nose pliers

Side cutters

Knotter tool

Craft glue

Scissors

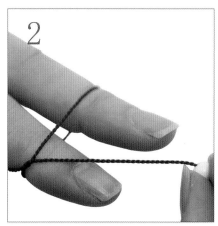

Bracelet

YOU WILL NEED

8 x 5mm opaque lamp beads, white

4 x large (28 x2 1mm) acrylic oval beads, blue and white

4 x 18mm acrylic round, blue and white

1 x 11¾in (300mm) length of elastic beading cord, thick black

Cut 11¾in (300mm) of elastic cord and thread the beads so that the round blue and oval blue bead alternate with glass white beads in between each bead. Pull the cord to gather up the beads and tie a few tight knots. Trim the excess cord. Add a dab of clear nail varnish to the knot to secure if you wish.

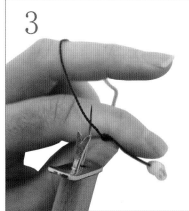

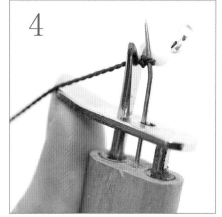

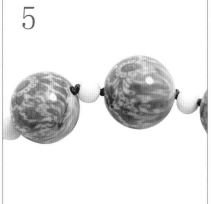

Necklace

1. Remove the silk cord from the card. Make a double knot in the end of the cord without the needle. Add a dab of glue to the knot and trim the excess silk. Place a calotte over the knot and squeeze closed with your pliers.

2. Thread a white glass bead onto the cord and move to the end. Make a loop around two fingers with silk thread—drop the end between your fingers to make a knot.

3. Insert the end of the prong into the loop (pointing away from your hand)—remove your fingers and tighten the knot on the prong.

4. Insert the silk into the Y-shaped part of the knotter tool. Pull the silk with your free hand so that the silk knot tightens on the prong. Keep hold of the silk with your free hand—with your thumb, push up on the knotter tool so the knot slips off the prong and sits snugly against the previous bead.

5. Next thread on a round blue bead and repeat the steps to make a knot next to the bead. Continue in this way so you have five round blue beads, sixteen ovals and five more round blue beads, all with a white glass bead between.

6. Make a double knot after the last white bead and add a calotte in the same way as the first. Add a jumpring to the loop of each calotte and squeeze the loops closed. Add a trigger clasp to one of the jumprings.

Earrings

YOU WILL NEED

2 x 32mm acrylic coin, blue and white

2 x 5mm glass beads, white

2 x headpins, silver-plated

2 x earwires, silver-plated

Thread a 5mm white glass bead, a blue coin, and a final white bead onto a headpin. Bend into a simple loop (see page 20), attach an earwire and close the loop. Repeat to make a pair.

Watch the Rainbow

Make this bright and vivid jewelry set, created by Lynn Allingham, which includes a watch face as part of the bracelet. The colorful buttons give these pieces a fun, nostalgic appeal.

FOR THE BRACELET YOU WILL NEED

1 x chunky double-link curb chain, silver

1 x quartz watch face, silver

1 x large lobster clasp, silver

1 x small curb chain, silver

1 x puffy heart charm, silver

1 x puffy heart charm, gunmetal silver

4 x small oval jumprings, silver

3 x strong 4mm jumprings, silver

40–50 x 7mm jumprings, silver (8mm if preferred)

Large selection of miniature buttons

Round-nose pliers

Side cutters

2 x flat-nose pliers

Be selective with your button colors. Always put three contrasting colors on each jumpring and try to keep them evenly spread to give a good rainbow effect.

Bracelet

1 Take the chunky double-link curb chain and cut it into two roughly 2½in (60mm) lengths. This size makes a small watch—the chain length can be tailored for specific wrist sizes.

2 Take a selection of small, brightly colored buttons and two 7mm jumprings for every link in the chain. For this size of watch you will need around 40–50 jumprings. Put three buttons on each jumpring, mixing the colors as desired (see page 16).

3 Start to attach the jumprings onto the chain. Attach two jumprings with three buttons to every link in the chain, one on each side.

4 Attach the two chain straps to the watch face using two small oval jumprings on each side. Using two jumprings to attach the straps can be fiddly, but do persevere.

5 Take a piece of small curb chain roughly 2in (50mm) in length and attach two puffy heart charms using a strong jumpring. Attach the chain to the end of the button strap using another strong jumpring. This acts as an extension chain for altering the size of the watch.

6 Take a large lobster clasp and attach the other end of the watch using a strong jumpring.

3

6

A good alternative to the puffy heart charms would be a pot-of-gold charm or a small gold coin to give the effect of finding a pot of gold at the end of a rainbow.

Earrings

YOU WILL NEED

2 x earwires

6 x miniature buttons

2 x puffy heart charms

8 x 5mm jumprings

2 x 6mm jumprings

1 x 10in (250mm) fine trace chain

Take three colored buttons and attach to three descending lengths of trace chain using a 5mm jumpring for each button (see page 16). Take one longer piece of chain and add a puffy heart charm using a 5mm ring. Place all four pieces together on a 6mm jumpring and attach to an earwire. Repeat to make a matching pair.

Hair clips

YOU WILL NEED

2 x large buttons

2 x pretty hair clips

E6000 glue

Make hair clips by attaching two large buttons to any type of hair clip. Use a strong glue.

Dream Catcher

Make this set of projects by Nicky Townsend, inspired by Native American tribes who believe that bad dreams are trapped in the dream catcher's web.

FOR THE NECKLACE YOU WILL NEED

10 x blue feathers approx. 3in (75mm) long

3 x feather charms

50 x 5mm wooden beads in blue, brown and cream

1 x small dream catcher, approx. 2in (50mm) in blue

1 x 30in (760mm) tan faux suede thong

13 x 5mm jumprings

2 x crimp beads

13 x flat ribbon cord ends

1 x roll of beading wire

3 x 2in (50mm) lengths of blue chain

1 x clasp

Strong glue

Flat-nose pliers

Scissors

Necklace

1 You can either make your own dreamcatcher or you can buy a readymade one and modify it, as shown here. First, remove the attachments on the dreamcatcher and replace them with the faux suede. Attach various lengths to the outer ring by folding the suede in half and taking the looped end through the ring of the dreamcatcher. Bring the cut ends through the looped end and pull tight. Tie three lengths to the bottom and one centrally at the top of the ring to use later to create the bail. Cut the ends level and clamp together with a ribbon end by placing the suede ends as close to the fold on the ribbon end and pressing the ribbon end closed. Dab a spot of glue inside the ribbon end before closing with flat-nose pliers for extra security.

2 Take a selection of feathers and trim off any long, sharp ends leaving enough to fit neatly into a ribbon-end clamp. Dab a couple of spots of glue inside a ribbon end then place feathers inside and using flat-nose pliers, clamp the ribbon end together. Repeat for six more feathers. To vary the look you can also thread some beads onto your feathers—choose beads with large holes, add a dab of glue to the base of the feather and slide the beads down to the glue. Finish with a ribbon end and attach a jumpring to each.

3 Measure out two 8in (200mm) lengths of faux suede, fold in half, and secure each end using a ribbon end. Again you can use a dab of glue inside the ribbon end for extra security. You will now have two finished pieces of faux suede that are 4in (100mm) in length. Measure out some beading wire to your preferred length and crimp securely to the loop in one end of one of the pieces of faux suede that you have just prepared.

4 You can now begin to thread on your beads. Thread them to about a quarter of the way along the length of wire and then thread on a feather that you prepared in Step 2. Thread on a few more beads and then another feather. Stop at the halfway point— you will continue to add the rest of the beads when you've prepared the bail on the dreamcatcher pendant. Put this section to one side for now.

5 Take your dreamcatcher and trim the ends of the central piece of faux suede at the top level. Dab a spot of glue inside a ribbon end and place the ends of faux suede in it then clamp together with flat-nose pliers. Attach a jumpring to the loop in the ribbon end. Take the half-threaded section from the last step and thread the dreamcatcher onto the wire. Continue threading on beads and two more feathers, then bead to the end. Finish off by crimping the wire to one end of the second piece of faux suede that you prepared earlier. Add a clasp.

6 Take the remaining three feathers and attach each to one of the three lengths of suede on the dreamcatcher pendant using jumprings. Measure three lengths of chain—each one should be roughly the same length as the feathers. Secure each piece of chain to the jumpring that attaches the feathers to the pendant—do this by opening the last link on the piece of chain, attach it to the jumpring, and then close the link back up. Finish off by adding a silver feather charm to the end of each piece of chain using a jumpring.

2

4

6

Earrings

YOU WILL NEED

6 x blue feathers approx. 3in (75mm) long

2 x feather charms

4 x 5mm jumprings

2 x flat ribbon cord ends

2 x 2in (50mm) lengths of blue chain

2 x earwires

Attach three feathers to each ribbon cord end, trimming as necessary to make them fit. Link the ribbon cord end to the earwire with a jumpring (see page 16), adding a chain piece onto the same jumpring before closing. Use the last two jumprings to place the feather charms on the ends of the chain.

Handbag charm

YOU WILL NEED

2 x blue feathers approx. 3in (75mm) long

2 x feather charms

7 x 5mm wooden beads in blue, brown and cream

1 x swivel clip keyring

1 x 4in (100mm) tan faux suede thong

4 x 5mm jumprings

1 x flat ribbon cord ends

2 x 2in (50mm) headpins

4 x 2in (50mm) lengths of blue chain

Attach the feathers together with a ribbon cord end. Make up beaded pieces on the headpins, one with three beads and the other with four beads, and make simple loops at the ends of the pins (see page 20). Take the keyring and place two suede pieces on it the same way as in Step 1 of the main project. Add the four pieces of chain by opening the end link on each piece of chain and adding it to the keyring. Add the leather charms and the two beaded headpins to the ends of the chains with jumprings (see page 16). Finally, add the feathers to the middle of the pieces now on the keyring with another jumpring.

Island Shores

Use linking techniques to create this jewelry set by Maggie Jones in colors inspired by the sea and seashore. The fluid style echoes moving tides and sea glass gathered on a beach walk.

FOR THE NECKLACE YOU WILL NEED

22 x 12mm round beads, banded agate

16 x 8mm round beads, green jasper

27 x 6mm potato pearls, blue

8 x 6mm baroque pearls, white

40 x 4mm round metal spacers, silver

34 x 4mm glass beads, frosted turquoise

8 x 6mm rondelles, clear

29 x 10mm octagonal discs, clear

3 x 4mm metal flower spacer beads

6 x cat's eye chips, orange

4 x pieces of sea glass

32 x 2in (50mm) eyepins, silver

6 x 2in (50mm) headpins, silver

8 x 4mm open jumprings, silver

28 x 4mm closed jumprings, silver

1 x roll of beading wire, nylon-covered

1 x roll of US 24-gauge (SWG 25, 0.5mm) wire, silver

2 x crimp tubes, silver

4 x 4in (100mm) fine-link chain, silver

1 x push-button clasp

Chain-nose pliers

You may find it easier to add a bare eyepin to the sea glass at Step 3, adding the pearls afterwards.

Use the image of the finished necklace to help you decide which beads to put on the droppers.

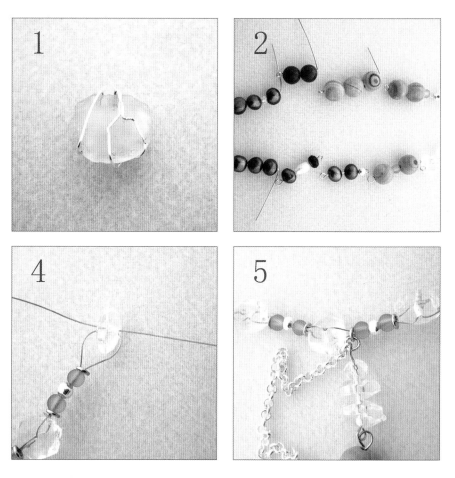

Necklace

1 Using silver-colored wire, wrap four pieces of sea glass. Go with the shape of the glass, settling the wire in any nicks or curves. Tuck in the ends on the reverse. To tighten the wire, twist chain-nose pliers on wire strands, making a "z" shape.

2 Create eight long droppers, two each of 3½in (90mm), 4⅓in (110mm), 4¾in (120mm), and 5⅛in (130mm). Lay out your design—blue pearls and occasional orange chips at the bottom, then 8mm rounds, agate, and finally crystal discs and rondelles at the top. Add random silver spacers, white pearls, and turquoise, frosted beads. When happy with the design, put each group of beads onto eyepins. Make a simple loop at the ends (see page 20) linking to the ones below and above.

3 On the bottom of four droppers, add the wire-wrapped sea glass directly to the loop of the eyepin, using wire on the edge of the glass, rather than the reverse.

4 For the neckband, cut two lengths of beading wire, each 23⅝in (600mm) long. Leave a ⁵⁄₁₆in (8mm) tail. Thread onto both strands a turquoise bead, and a closed jumpring, then thread a disc by passing each wire through in opposite directions. Return to using both strands and thread the jumpring, a turquoise bead, and a silver spacer. Repeat this pattern a further 13 times, then finish with a turquoise bead, a jumpring, a disc, and a final turquoise bead.

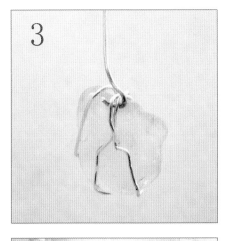

3

6

Earrings

YOU WILL NEED

2 x 6mm potato pearls, blue

4 x 6mm baroque pearls, white

2 x 2in (50mm) eyepins, silver

2 x 2in (50mm) headpins, silver

2 x earwires

Round-nose pliers

Place a baroque pearl on each headpin and create a simple loop at the ends (see page 20) using round-nose pliers. Attach the loop to the end of an eyepin and thread on a potato pearl then another baroque parl, finish the pin with another simple loop. Attach to the earwire with this loop. Make a second one exactly the same for a pair.

Hair accessory

YOU WILL NEED

3 x 12mm round beads, banded agate

4 x 6mm potato pearls, blue

1 x 6mm baroque pearls, white

2 x 4mm round metal spacers, silver

1 x cat's eye chips, orange

3 x 2in (50mm) eyepins, silver

1 x 2in (50mm) headpins, silver

1 x 4mm open jumprings, silver

1 x 6mm jumpring

1 x hair stick with loop end

Give your up-do a touch of Eastern glamour! Create droppers as in the main necklace and use a 6mm jumpring to attach to the top loop of a hair stick.

5   Attach the droppers to the closed jumprings on the neckband using open jumprings. Slide four individual white pearls onto headpins, make wrapped loops and attach each to lengths of chain, between 3–4in (8–10cm) long. Distribute throughout the beaded links, attaching to the jumprings.

6   On each end of the neckband, attach a closed jumpring, using crimps with a silver spacer bead in between (see page 21). Don't squash the crimps yet—check first for a good fit. Add the fastener components to each side using jumprings.

Chainmaille Spiral

This beautiful set by Gemma Reilly uses a simple chainmaille technique that incorporates gold twist beads and oval jumprings.

FOR THE NECKLACE YOU WILL NEED

20 x black and gold twist beads

35 x 4mm oval jumprings, gold-colored

55 x 5mm oval jumprings, gold-colored

152 x 6mm oval jumprings, gold-colored

20 x eyepins, gold-colored

1 x ⅝in (15mm) trigger clasp, gold-colored

Round-nose pliers

Chain-nose pliers

Necklace

1 To make the longest length of chain, open 79 (6mm) jumprings, 30 (5mm) jumprings and 20 (4mm) jumprings (see page 16). This will make it much easier to add each link.

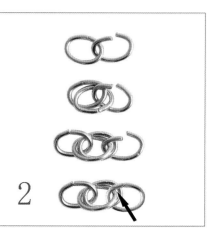

2 Pick up a closed 6mm jumpring. Add an open 6mm jumpring and close. Add another jumpring to the two jumprings and close. Pass another jumpring through the end two jumprings and close. The easiest way to add the jumprings is to hold the chain flat between your thumb and forefinger, as this makes it easier to see the end two jumprings. Continue in the same way, adding a new jumpring to the two previous ones.

3 It takes 10–20 jumprings to be joined together for the pattern to emerge. When you have added all of the 6mm jumprings, continue with the 5mm and finally the 4mm to create a tapered spiral chain. Make a second chain using 75 (6mm), 25 (5mm) and 15 (4mm) jumprings.

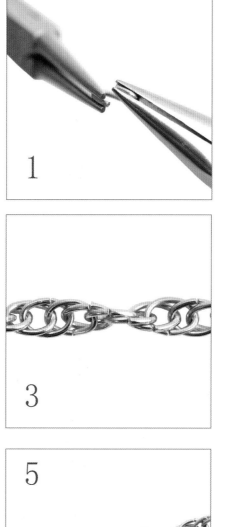

4 Thread a bead onto an eyepin; trim the eyepin ⅜in (10mm) above the bead. Bend into a loop (see page 20) and add another eyepin close the loop. Repeat to make two lengths of ten beads.

5 Open a 6mm jumpring and attach the two largest ends of the chains to one of the beaded sections. To smooth out the spiral twist each end of the chain in opposite directions. Attach the smaller ends of the chain in the same way to the second beaded section.

6 Add an oval jumpring with a trigger clasp to one end of the beaded section and an oval jumpring to the other end.

Bracelet

YOU WILL NEED

4 x black and gold twist beads

27 x 6mm oval jumprings, gold-colored

4 x eyepins, gold-colored

1 x ⅝in (15mm) trigger clasp, gold-colored

Add a trigger clasp to an oval jumpring, add a second oval jumpring and close. Add an eyepin to the second jumpring, thread on a bead, trim ⅜in (10mm) above the bead, bend into a loop, add a jumpring, and close. Make a spiral in the same way as the main project, using eight jumprings. Add a beaded eyepin. Continue until the bracelet is the desired length. Add a couple of single jumprings at the end of the bracelet.

Leave out the beaded section for a simple twisted chain—just attach the clasp to one end of the chain section.

This style of chainmaille design works really well with oval jumprings but it can also be achieved with round rings.

Earrings

YOU WILL NEED

6 x black and gold twist beads

4 x eyepins, gold-colored

2 x headpins, gold-colored

2 x earwires, gold-colored

Thread a bead onto a headpin. Trim ⅜in (10mm) above the bead, bend into a loop, and add an eyepin. Close the loop. Add another bead and a final beaded eyepin in the same way. Attach an earwire to the final eyepin. Repeat to make a pair.

Castaway

Create this beautifully textured set of projects by Beth Reeves, which exudes the laid-back style of a Thai beach.

FOR THE NECKLACE YOU WILL NEED

11 x black pearls

2 x small tube beads, patterned

2 x heavy beads, metal decorated

2 x shell discs, round tigris

2 x shell discs, mother-of-pearl

2 x two-holed rings

11 x cultured pearls, pink

4 x small leaf-shaped charms

10 x small nuggets, champagne

18 x natural shell bead, trucha

9 x lava round beads

18 x tiny cushion beads

14 x natural buttons

4 x small pebble beads, white opaque

1 x natural leather thong

1 x 79in (2m) length of thin natural cotton cord

30 x small jumprings, gold

2 x cord ends, gold-colored

24 x thin headpins, gold

4 x eyepins, gold

Chain-nose pliers

Scissors

Necklace

Earrings

YOU WILL NEED

2 x two-holed gold discs

2 x cultured pearls, pink

4 x natural shell bead, trucha

4 x small jumprings, gold

2 x headpins, gold

2 x eyepins, gold

2 x earwires

Thread a pearl onto a headpin and turn a loop to attach to an eyepin (see page 20). Thread on two shell beads, turn a loop, and attach a gold two-holed disc. Fix an earring hook with a small jumpring.

1 Put the shell discs, two-holed rings, and larger metal beads to one side. Place the black pearls, freshwater pearls, and white pebble beads onto thin headpins and turn a wrapped loop (see page 18). At the top of each loop attach a small jumpring. Now add jumprings to each leaf. Save one black pearl and one pink pearl for the end of the necklace.

2 Cut your thin cord in half. Roughly divide your remaining smaller beads into two piles (lava beads, stick shells, buttons, champagne nuggets, and tiny gold beads). Divide your bead clusters in half, too. Take one strand and tie a knot 2in (50mm) from the end. Thread on beads from one pile, knotting after each one in a random design.

3 The buttons and shells work best grouped in pairs. After every couple of beads thread on a cluster until the necklace is around 7in (180mm) in length. Repeat Step 2 with the second piece of cord until you have two fully beaded strands, one slightly shorter than the other. Lay the two strands next to each other and check your clusters do not overlap.

4 Join the two strands together at each end of the necklace with a knot followed by the large patterned gold bead. Knot after the bead. On one side of the necklace attach a small cord end just above the gold bead with a pair of chain-nose pliers (see page 18). Cut away any excess cord. Repeat on the other side.

5 Attach one side of the two-holed ring to the folding crimp with a small jumpring. Fix the other side to an eyepin and thread on one of your shell discs. Turn a basic loop and attach another jumpring, linking to a second eyepin with the second shell disc. Finish with a loop and final jumpring.

6 Cut the leather thong in half. Thread one piece through the jumpring at the top of the necklace. Slide the metal tube bead over both strands to hold in place. Join both ends together with one cord end and finish with a jumpring and one of your remaining dangling pearls. Repeat on the other side.

1

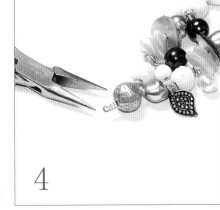

2

3

4

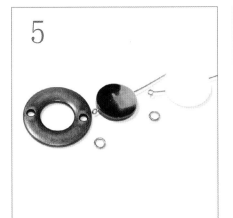

5

6

Bracelet

YOU WILL NEED

16 x mix of black pearls, pink cultured pearls, white opaque small pebble beads

16 x headpins, gold

16 x 4mm jumprings, gold

6 x 15mm jumprings, gold

12 x mix of large beads, lava, shell and metal

Elastic cord

Place ten pearls on headpins, making simple loops at the ends (see page 20), and thread onto a jumpring. Repeat to make three clusters. Using three large jumprings, make a Russian knot by attaching two jumprings together then place a third ring through the two already attached together. Make two. Using pearls and pebble beads create six dangles on headpins and attach to a jumpring, or a drop connector. Choose some pale, chunky beads to match and thread the beads onto elastic, interspersed with the clusters and dangles. Tie the elastic in several knots to complete.

Pearls & Spikes

Embrace the two hottest trends on the planet—spikes and rose gold—with these tactile and quirky pieces by Gill Teasdale.

FOR THE NECKLACE YOU WILL NEED

2 x calottes, antique silver

1 x hook and fastener, antique copper

41 x acrylic spikes

20 x 2mm spacer rounds, antique silver

1 x 59in (1.5m) length of black beading thread

2 x size 11 colored seed beads

82 x 3mm pearls, rose gold

8 x 10mm pearls, rose gold

56 x 4mm crystals, rose gold

4 x 4mm rounds, rose gold

38 x 4mm rounds, jet

14 x 6mm rounds, rose gold

4 x 11mm pendant drops, jet

6 x 5mm jumprings, silver-plated

8 x $^{13}/_{16}$in (20mm) eyepins, silver-plated

Beading glue

Thread conditioner (optional)

Beading needle

Chain-nose pliers

Round-nose pliers

Side cutters

Scissors

Necklace

1 Condition the thread before knotting a seed bead securely onto one end and trimming the tail. Thread the needle on the other end. Pass the thread fully through a calotte, from the inside out, so that the seed bead sits in the cup of the calotte. Begin threading on beads following the next steps, keeping each section tight and being careful not to allow the thread to tangle.

2 Thread a pearl, a jet round, a 4mm rose gold round, a jet round, a pearl, and a crystal. Repeat the sequence twice, the second time using a 6mm rose gold round instead of 4mm. Thread a spike, a crystal, a pearl, a jet round, a 6mm rose gold round, a jet round, a pearl, and a crystal. Repeat this sequence twice, omitting the last crystal on the second repeat.

3 Thread a jet round, a 6mm rose gold round, a jet round, a spacer, five pearls, and a spacer. Pass the needle back through the jet, rose gold, and jet rounds in the same direction. Thread a spacer, four pearls, a drop, four pearls, and a spacer. Pass the thread back through the same three rounds then thread another pearl. Thread a crystal and a spike. Repeat twice. Thread a crystal and a pearl.

4 Repeat Step 3 three times, so you have a row of four double-looped pieces with a drop in the middle and rows of three spikes in between. On the last repeat, omit the spike section after the fourth double loop. Complete the rest of the pattern to match the other side created in Step 2 (reversing the instructions). Add a calotte, threading it on from the outside. Thread a seed bead, pass the needle back down through the seed bead and the cover, leaving a large loop of thread at least 4in (100mm) long.

5 Pass the needle back down the last two beads and then back up the last pearl (bypassing the round), then on back through the hinge. Keeping the 4in (100mm) tail separate, pull through the excess thread. Remove the needle and tie the doubled 4in (100mm) tail and the single long thread in a double knot around the seed bead. Trim the ends close to the knot.

6 Add a dot of glue to each knot. When dry, squeeze both the calottes closed with chain-nose pliers. Hook the open loop on one of the calottes through the loop on one of the hook parts. Close the loop securely using chain-nose pliers. Make sure there is no gap or the end fastener may slip out. Repeat with the other calotte and fastener part.

Use the open-and-close-a-jumpring technique on page 20, as reference for opening eyepin loops.

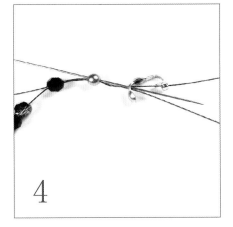

Earrings

YOU WILL NEED

2 x fandangles, antique silver

2 x earwires, antique silver

6 x acrylic spikes

6 x 2in (50mm) eyepins, antique silver

6 x 5mm jumprings, antique silver

18 x 4mm faceted round beads

2 x 6mm faceted round beads

4 x size 11 seed beads

Attach all the spikes to eyepins using jumprings. Add three beads to each eyepin and create a simple loop (see page 20) at the top of each pin. Attach these loops to the bottom of the two fandangles, with one on each outer section and the other in the middle. Attach the top of the fandangles to the leftover eyepins. Add a seed bead with a 6mm bead in the middle to each eyepin and create simple loops at the top. Attach these to earwires to complete the earrings.

Bracelet

YOU WILL NEED

1 x 11¾in (300mm) length of 0.7mm elastic beading cord, clear

24 x acrylic spikes

16 x 4mm crystals

8 x 10mm pearls

String 10mm pearls and clusters of three spikes spaced with crystals onto stretchy beading wire for a fun bracelet. Knot the elastic a few times to secure and cut off the excess.

Resources

UK

Beads Unlimited
Stockwell Lodge Studios
Rear of 121-131
Conway Street
Hove
East Sussex
BN3 3LW
Tel: +44 (0)1273 740777
www.beadsunlimited.co.uk

Beads Direct Ltd
10 Duke Street
Loughborough
Leicestershire
LE11 1ED
Tel: +44 (0)1509 218028
www.beadsdirect.co.uk

The Bead Shop
44 Higher Ardwick
Manchester
M12 6DA
Tel: +44 (0)161 274 4040
www.the-beadshop.co.uk

Fred Aldous Ltd
37 Lever Street
Manchester
M1 1LW
Tel: +44 (0)161 236 4224
www.fredaldous.co.uk

Bead and Button Company
The Workshop
58 Lower North Road
Carnforth
Lancashire
LA5 9LJ
Tel: +44 (0)1524 720 880
www.beadandbuttoncompany.
co.uk

Palmer Metals Ltd
401 Broad Lane
Coventry
CV5 7AY
Tel: +44 (0)845 644 9343
www.palmermetals.co.uk

Spoilt Rotten Beads
7 The Green,
Haddenham
Ely
Cambridgeshire
CB6 3TA
Tel: +44 (0)1353 749853
www.spoiltrottenbeads.co.uk

Jillybeads
1 Anstable Road
Morecambe
LA4 6TG
Tel: +44 (0)1524 412728
www.jillybeads.co.uk

The Bead Merchant
22 Observer way
Kelvedon
Essex
CO5 9NZ
Tel: +44 (0)1376 570022
www.beadmerchant.co.uk

Bead Aura
3 Neal's Yard
Covent Garden
London
WC2H 9DP
Tel: +44 (0)20 7836 3002
www.beadaura.co.uk

The Genuine Gemstone
Company Limited
Unit 2D Eagle Road
Moons Moat
Redditch
Worcestershire
B98 9HF
Tel: +44 (0)800 6444 655
www.jewellerymaker.com

Creative BeadCraft
Unit 2 Asheridge Business
Centre
Asheridge Road
Chesham
Buckinghamshire
HP5 2PT
Tel: +44 (0)1494 778818
www.creativebeadcraft.co.uk

Beadtime
Beadtime Warehouse
Unit 16, Shepperton Business
Park
Govett Avenue
Shepperton
TW17 8BA
Tel: +44 (0)1932 244700
www.beadtime.co.uk

Bijoux Beads
Elton House
2 Abbey Street
Bath
BA1 1NN
Tel: +44 (0)1225 482024
www.bijouxbeads.co.uk

GJ Beads
Unit L
St Erth Industrial Estate
Hayle
Cornwall
TR27 6LP
Tel: +44 (0)1736 751070
www.gjbeads.co.uk

Beadsisters
Mid Cairngarroch Croft
Stoneykirk
Stranraer
Wigtownshire
DG9 9EH
Tel: +44 (0)1776 830352
www.beadsisters.co.uk

Shiney Rocks
14 Sandy Park Road,
Brislington
Bristol
BS4 3PE
Tel: +44 (0)117 300 9800
www.shineyrocks.co.uk

Wires.co.uk
Unit 3 Zone A
Chelmsford Road Industrial
Estate
Great Dunmow
Essex
CM6 1HD
Tel: +44 (0)1371 238013
www.wires.co.uk

USA

Beadin' Path
Tel: +1 207-650-1557
www.beadinpath.com

Fire Mountain Gems
and Beads
1 Fire Mountain Way
Grants Pass
OR 97526-2373
Tel: +1 800-355-2137
(toll free)
Tel: +1 541-956-7890
www.firemountaingems.com

Vintaj Natural Brass
Company
PO box 246
Galena, Il 61036
www.vintaj.com

Index

To place an order, or to request a catalogue, contact:

GMC Publications Ltd

Castle Place, 166 High Street, Lewes, East Sussex, BN7 1XU

United Kingdom

Tel: +44 (0)1273 488005

Website: www.gmcbooks.com